The 2020 Jacob D. Maendel Lectures

"Holding Fast to What is Good?"
Tradition and Renewal in Hutterite History

Astrid von Schlachta
translated by Jesse Hofer

© 2020 Astrid von Schlachta

All rights reserved. No part of this publication may be reproduced, stored in a retrieval system, or transmitted in any form or by any means without the prior written permission of the publisher.

Bible quotations are taken from the New Revised Standard Version. Used by permission.

Cover Image: Title page of the so-called *"Allgemeine Dienst Ordnung"* located in the Bruderhof Historical Archives, Walden, New York (EAH 165).

The artistic representation of Jacob D. Maendel used for the Jacob D. Maendel Lectures logo was designed by Brendan Maendel.

ISSN 2562-7481

PRINT ISBN: 978-1-927913-96-3
E-BOOK ISBN: 978-1-998141-00-5

Library and Archives Canada Cataloguing in Publication
Title: "Holding fast to what is good?" : tradition and renewal in Hutterite history / Astrid von Schlachta ; translated by Jesse Hofer.
Names: Schlachta, Astrid von, author.
Description: Series statement: The 2020 Jacob D. Maendel Lectures, 2562-7481 | Lectures presented via live-streaming, June 6, 13, 20, and 27, 2020 from the Mennonitische Forschungsstelle in Weierhof, Germany. | Translated from the German.
Identifiers: Canadiana 20210140569 | ISBN 9781927913963 (softcover)
Subjects: LCSH: Hutterian Brethren—History.
Classification: LCC BX8129.H8 S34 2021 | DDC 289.7/3—dc23

Box 40 • MacGregor, MB • R0H 0R0
p. 204-272-5132 • f. 204-252-2381 • e. orders@hbbookcentre.com

Printed in Canada.

The 2020
Jacob D. Maendel Lectures
were presented via live-streaming
from the Mennonitische Forschungsstelle
in Weierhof, Germany
on June 6, 13, 20, and 27, 2020.

TABLE OF CONTENTS

Introduction -- I

LECTURE I
"It is only in good order that something can be created…"? ------ 1

LECTURE II
"Test everything and hold fast to what is good." ------------------ 23

LECTURE III
"How can we accept a government authority among us?" ------- 47

LECTURE IV
"We do not wish nor desire to do harm or evil to any man."---- 79

Conclusion --- 97

About Jacob D. Maendel ---101

About Astrid von Schlachta -------------------------------------103

INTRODUCTION

When plans were initially made for the 2020 instalment of the Jacob D. Maendel Lectures, the intent was to gather in a physical space for three closely-scheduled lectures. This would have made sense if Dr. Astrid von Schlachta had come to Manitoba from Europe to deliver the lectures. These plans were altered when it became clear that the global coronavirus pandemic would not permit international travel and that gatherings of any kind were ill-advised. With this reality on our doorstep, we changed course and wondered what new opportunities might present themselves within a digital-only format. Our planning discussions via Zoom quickly identified an appropriate topic and four distinct periods, or pivot points. With the limitations of space and travel removed, we realized that hosting four lectures spread over the month of June would provide participants with the rich opportunity to reflect on the lecture during the week before listening to the next one.

The second instalment of the Jacob D. Maendel Lecture Series was, therefore, a four-part journey through the nearly-500-year history of the Hutterite movement. In each of the lectures, questions were raised about the implications of tradition versus renewal. These glimpses into the past made it clear that there were instances where tradition propelled the Hutterites forward, but other instances where firmly or uncritically clinging to traditions hindered community life.

The following questions guided the development of each lecture: First, how and when did Hutterites debate tradition versus renewal? Second, how did the political and social conditions affect Hutterite life and the foundations of their faith? And finally, what does this account of history have to teach us today about what it means to be a vibrant church that cherishes its past and traditions, while at the same time constantly reflecting on how and where renewal might be needed? The hope was that listeners (and now readers) will pose the question to themselves, "Do we dare to make costly choices? Do we dare to challenge beloved traditions that have outlived their usefulness? Do we dare…"

The vision of the Jacob D. Maendel Lectures is to bring the academic fields of history, theology, and literature, broadly conceived, under the discipline of, and into the service of the Church. In other words, the scholarship presented is to be of high calibre, but not merely an academic exercise for its own sake. Rather, the scholarship is to have direct ecclesiological implications, in the spirit of the motto, "*Ecclesia semper reformanda est* [the church must always be reformed]." The church can and must learn from the academy and, in turn, offer a witness and a prophetic critique to the academy and the wider world.

We are grateful to Dr. Astrid von Schlachta in helping us abundantly accomplish this lofty goal in the 2020 lectures. This publication is an expanded adaptation of the lectures she presented. The lectures were written in her native German and translated into English by Jesse Hofer.

Kenny Wollmann & Jesse Hofer
December 2020

LECTURE ONE
"It is only in good order that something can be created…"?[1]

In his 2019 Jacob D. Maendel Lectures, Ian Kleinsasser quoted from a presentation delivered by Hans Decker at an annual Hutterite German teachers' conference: "The drive to earn money has taken control to such an extent that spiritual responsibilities are pushed to the side."[2] Hans Decker referred primarily to the situation in the Hutterite schools, yet his statement points to a recurring theme in Hutterite history.

The Anabaptists

The Hutterites belong to the 16th century Anabaptist movement, which is itself a branch of the Reformation.[3] Many people who later became Anabaptists were at first followers of Martin Luther (Wittenberg) or Ulrich Zwingli (Zürich). They agreed with the Reformers that humans are not saved through works, but through the grace of God. No priest or pastor can mediate salvation, but only faith in Jesus Christ. The Anabaptists and other Reformers were convinced that each person must make a personal faith commitment and should read the Bible for themselves. They demanded a mature Christian life, characterized by an autonomous and confident faith.[4]

---

1 Rudolf Wolkan, ed., *Das große Geschichtbuch der Hutterischen Brüder* (Macleod/Wien, 1923), 335.
2 Ian Kleinsasser, *Blessings and Burdens: 100 Years of Hutterites in Manitoba* (MacGregor: Hutterian Brethren Book Centre, 2019), 22.
3 Nicole Grochowina, *Reformation* (Berlin/Boston: De Gruyter Oldenbourg, 2020); Thomas Kaufmann, *Erlöste und Verdammte: Eine Geschichte der Reformation* (München: C.H. Beck), 2016.
4 John D. Roth and James M. Stayer, eds., *A Companion to Anabaptism and Spirit-*

A 16th-century drawing, spread over two folios, combines two scenes into one: the right side the authorities discovery a nocturnal assembly of Anabaptists and the left side shows the two missioners being lead away into captivity. [SOURCE: Zentralbibliothek Zürich, Ms. F 23, fol. 394.]

However, the Anabaptists criticized Luther and Zwingli for relying on political support for the implementation of their spiritual reforms. For their part, the Anabaptists aimed to be as independent as possible from the influence of princely and city governments. Moreover, they did not agree with Luther and Zwingli's understanding of baptism; both of them retained infant baptism, while the Anabaptists only considered adult baptism based on a confession of faith as biblical.

In early Anabaptist circles, the motivation to read and interpret the Bible for oneself was high. In Switzerland and the Tyrol they created reading circles where believers gathered to discuss current developments, read and interpret the Bible together, and to pray. According to the sources, the Anabaptists were alert and critical readers for their time. They are repeatedly described as mature Christians who made up their own minds about the spiritual, social, and political circumstances of their time.[5]

---

ualism, 1521–1700 (Leiden/Boston: Brill, 2007); Astrid von Schlachta, Täufer: Von der Reformation ins 21. Jahrhundert (Tübingen: Narr Francke Attempto, 2020).

5   Andrea Strübind, Eifriger als Zwingli: Die frühe Täuferbewegung in der Schweiz (Berlin: Duncker & Humblot, 2003), esp. 129–147; Werner O. Packull, Hutterite Beginnings: Communitarian Experiments during the Reformation (Baltimore/London: Johns Hopkins University Press, 1995), esp. 171–186.

A Variety of Anabaptists

The Anabaptist movement of the 16th century was very colourful and diverse. Although all Anabaptists practiced adult or believer's baptism, they did not all agree on every theological point. Hutterites, the Swiss Brethren, and Mennonites were the main Anabaptist groups which emerged in the early 16th century. While the Hutterites settled mainly in the Tyrol and Moravia, the Swiss Brethren established communities in an area stretching from Switzerland to southwestern Germany and the Palatinate. The Mennonites lived in northern Germany and in the Netherlands. Many smaller groups and communities existed in the early years, but they disappeared in the course of the 16th century.

The theological diversity of these groups is apparent in the different congregational descriptions.[6] With their community-of-goods, the Hutterites represented the most intensive form of community life. Very different views, however, existed about other Anabaptist principles, such as non-resistance, attitudes towards political authorities, and government positions. We will revisit this topic in a later lecture.

The Anabaptists in the Tyrol

In the Tyrol, the persecution of Anabaptists was significantly more severe than in other parts of the Holy Roman Empire of the German Nation.[7] For that reason, it was not possible for the Anabaptists to establish communities there. The migration to Moravia offered an escape route—a road that many Tirolean Anabaptists took. In Moravia very tolerant lords provided the Hutterites with land which had been depopulated in the 15th century by a number of plagues. This was a relationship where both parties benefited: the lords needed subjects to resettle their lands and the Anabaptists were a good fit; for the Anabaptists, the situation in Moravia appeared to be a "paradise on earth." This initial situation provided

---

[6] Hans-Jürgen Goertz, *Die Täufer: Geschichte und Deutung*, 2nd ed. (München: C.H. Beck, 1988); von Schlachta, *Täufer*, esp. 113–147.

[7] Werner O. Packull, *Die Hutterer in Tirol: Frühes Täufertum in der Schweiz, Tirol und Mähren* (Innsbruck: Universitätsverlag Wagner, 1996); Astrid von Schlachta, Ellinor Forster, and Giovanni Merola, eds., *Verbrannte Visionen? Erinnerungsorte der Täufer in Tirol* (Innsbruck: Innsbruck University Press, 2007).

the conditions for the establishment and favourable development of the Hutterite community in Moravia.

Above all, it was thanks to Jakob Huter that many Tirolean Anabaptists settled in Moravia. Huter originated from the Puster Valley, which is located in South Tyrol today. He traveled tirelessly between the Tyrol and Moravia, accompanying refugees and preaching the Anabaptist faith.[8] The government organized many efforts to capture him and at the end of 1535, they were successful. On February 1536, Jakob Huter was burned at the stake in Innsbruck in front of *das Goldene Dachl*. Huter had given the community in Moravia its essential orientation and direction: he was the first *Ältester* of note, was the principal organizer of the migrations out of the Tyrol, and eventually became the namesake for his community.

The Hutterite *Bruderhöfe* in Moravia

Due to its favourable conditions, the 'Land in the East' became an attraction for the Anabaptists. In the course of the 16th century, many of them moved to Moravia and joined the Hutterites.

The number of Hutterite *Bruderhöfe* in Moravia grew during the 16th century as new ones were regularly established. In 1589 there were 57 *Bruderhöfe* or *Haushaben* on 25 estates, each with an average of 400 inhabitants. Undoubtedly these numbers were significantly higher during times of crisis, when a *Hof* had to be abandoned and its people accommodated by other communities. By 1600 there may have been as many as 20,000–25,000 Hutterites in South Moravia, which would have represented 2.5% of the region's population. Other sources indicate that 10% of the population was Hutterite.[9]

---

8 Hans Georg Fischer, "Jakob Huter – sein Leben und Wirken: ein Zeugnis evangelischer Frömmigkeit im 16. Jahrhundert," PhD diss., (Universität Wien, 1949).
9 Frantisek Hrubý, *Die Wiedertäufer in Mahren*. Sonderdruck aus dem *Archiv für Reformationsgeschichte* 30–32 (Leipzig: M. Heinsius Nachfolger, 1935); Thomas Winkelbauer, "Die Vertreibung der Hutterer aus Mähren 1622: Massenexodus oder Abzug der letzten Standhaften?" *Mennonitische Geschichtsblätter*, 61 (2004), 65–96; in general: Astrid von Schlachta, *From the Tyrol to North America: The Hutterite Story through the Centuries* (Kitchener: Pandora Press, 2008); Astrid von Schlachta, "Täufergemeinschaften: Die Hutterer," in *Europäische Geschichte Online*, (Institut für Europäische Geschichte, Mainz, 2011), http://www.ieg-ego.eu/schlachtaa-2011-de.

Buildings at Neumühl. [SOURCE: Mennonitische Forschungsstelle Weierhof.]

Neumühl and Nikolsburg were the administrative centres of Hutterite life. We get a glimpse of Hutterite life at this time from a copperplate print which appeared on the cover of a polemical text produced by the Catholic theologian Christoph Erhard in 1589. The book soundly vilified the Hutterites.

The Hutterites lived in large buildings, several of which comprised each community. They slept as a community in common rooms, separated by couples, single brothers, and sisters. Children slept at the schools, which were similar to present-day boarding schools. The Hutterites of the 16th century operated exemplary schools; the instruction was so progressive and of such a high calibre that even non-Hutterites sent their children to be instructed there. This boarding school system not only guarantee a good education, but also ensured that the women could work in the community all day. The copperplate found on the cover of Christoph Erhard's book provides the interesting detail that 16th century Hutterites apparently lived in dwellings with crown glass windows [*Butzenfenster*]. This is indicative of wealth because this type of window was expensive.

Economically, the Hutterites of the 16th century were employed as craftsmen, which another copperplate print portrays beautifully.

"Holding Fast to What is Good?"

Gründliche kurtz verfaste Historia.
Von Münsterischen Wi-
dertauffern: vnd wie die Hutterischen Brüder
so auch billich Widertauffer genent werden / im Löblichen
Marggraffthumb Märbern / deren vber die sibentzeben tausent sein
sollen/gedachten Münsterischen in vilen änhlich/
gleichformig vnd mit zustimmet sein.

Durch.
Christoffen Erhard Theologum, auß der Fürstlichen
Graffschafft Tyrol/von Hall gebern.

Gedruckt zu München/Bey Adam Berg.
Cum gratia & priuilegio Cæs: May:
Anno M. D. LXXXVIIII.

Title page of *Gründliche kurtz verfaste Historia von Münsterischen Widertauffern* by Christoph Erhard. In English the full title reads, "A Comprehensive and Brief Compiled History of Münster's Anabaptists: And how the Hutterian Brethren in the Noble Margraviate of Moravia are also rightly to be considered Anabaptist, whose [population] is said to be over seventeen thousand. [They are] similar to the Münsterites in many respects, and in agreement with them." [SOURCE: Munich, 1589. A copy is available in the Mennonite Historical Library at Goshen College, Indiana.]

Der Hutterischen Widertauffer Taubenkobel:

In welchem all jhre Wüst / Mist / Kott vnnd Vnflat / das ist / ihr falsche / stinckende / vnflätige vnd abscheuliche Lehrn / was sie nemblich von Gott / von Christo / von den H. Sacramenten vnd andern Artickeln deß Christlichen Glaubens halten / werden erzählet / alle kürtzlich vnd treulich auß ihren eygnen Büchern / so wol getruckten als geschribnen / mit Anzeygung deß Orths / wo ein jedtliche zufinden / verfasset.

Auch deß grossen Taubers deß Jacob Hutters Leben / von welchem sich die Widertauffer Hutterisch nennen / angehencket:

Durch CHRISTOPHORVM ANDREAM Fischer D.
Pfarrherrn zu Velsperg.

Mit Röm: Kay|: Mayest: Freyheit.
Getruckt zu Ingolstatt / in der Ederischen Truckerey /
Durch Andream Angermeyr.

ANNO M. DC. VII.

Title page of *Der Hutterischen Wiedertauffer Taubenkobel* by Christoph Andreas Fischer, 1607. In English the full title reads, "The Hutterite Anabaptist Pigeoncote: In which all their Waste, Shit, Dung, and Filth, that is, their false, stinking, filthy, and abominable teachings that they believe regarding God, Christ, the Holy Sacraments, and other articles of the Christian faith are articulated—briefly and faithfully from their own publications, both printed and handwritten—with citations to indicate where everything can be found. Also, [an account] of the great cock pigeon Jacob Hutter's life, after whom the Anabaptist Hutterites name themselves, appended." [SOURCE: Ingolstadt, 1607.]

It appeared in 1607 on the cover of an equally polemical text by Christoph Andreas Fischer depicting a dovecote. The trades practiced by the Hutterites are symbolized by figures and objects suspended on the perches jutting out of the dovecote.

A variety of trades were found in the communities: carpenters, saddlers, blacksmiths, knife makers, potters, stove builders, shoemakers, millers, tailors, and many more. The Hutterites also had barber-surgeons [*Bader*] and doctors among them. With their trades and high-quality products, the Hutterites gained recognition and prominence beyond the borders of Moravia. Their customers included both the nobility and burghers [*Bürger*], who also benefitted from the services of the Hutterite doctors. One of the Hutterite doctors, Georg Zobel, was employed by the Emperor's court in Prague when Emperor Rudolf II resided there. At the same time, Hutterites also practiced agriculture, though on a much smaller scale than their manufacturing work and mostly for their own use. A look at the economy of the Hutterites in Moravia shows that from the middle of the 16th century onward, they were no longer "the persecuted ones;" rather, they were well-respected, produced quality goods, and were considered to be reliable business partners.

The Spiritual Life of the Hutterites and Offices in the Community

Very early on, a group of elders designated as the "respected ones" [*Fürnehme*] or elders [*Ältesten*] was formed to make the most important decisions in the communities. Peter Riedemann mentions this group in his *Rechenschaft* published in the mid-1540s:

> Finally, there are elders, who serve in the church wherever and however need requires. They work with the servants to consider diligently the needs of the church community and to promote its well-being. In this way they help the servants bear the burden so that the whole church does not need to be concerned with every small matter.[10]

---

10   Peter Riedemann, *Rechenschaft unsrer Religion, Lehre und Glaubens* ([Berne]: Verlag der Huterischen Brüder Gemeine, 1902), 78.

According to Peter Riedemann, the elders of the community were also considered servants of the church.

Who were the elders? Who belonged to their circle? We know that in the second half of the 16th century the ministers [*Diener des Worts*] and occasionally also the stewards [*Haushalter*] belonged to this circle. At any rate, at the broader church level there was both an *Ältester* and a body of elders. Together they were responsible for leading the church community. Among other things, they made decisions about the appointment of ministers and stewards, the filling of other important positions, community regulations, administring the ban and reacceptance, as well as deciding where to send missionaries. Beyond this, every community had their own leadership team, described in one source as the rulers or regents [*Regenten*]. The steward, the head waiter, the vineyard tender [*Weinzierl*] and several leaders of the trades were part of this team.[11]

In the early years, the Servants of the Word were chosen by lot. Later, it appears that appointing ministers became the norm. The sources specify that the elders should be notified when a new Servant of the Word is needed and the elders should discuss and consider who could be called to this position. Both the ministers and also the stewards were first named to the position for about two years and then confirmed in their service.

Hutterites gathered each Sunday and Wednesday for *Lehr*, where two or three brothers preached in succession. According to the ordinances, Sunday was to be honoured and celebrated, but that one's personal piety should not be dependent on a single day of the week. Rather, faith should be lived throughout the week. Since the *Ältester* participated in all Lord's Supper observations, they took place at different times throughout the year. Easter, Pentecost, and Christmas were observed as church holidays by the Hutterites.

From the beginning, and throughout the 16th century, Hutterites carried out intensive missionary work. Each spring the community sent out missionaries to various regions of the Old Empire. They

---

11 Astrid von Schlachta, *Hutterische Konfession und Tradition (1578–1619): Etabliertes Leben zwischen Ordnung und Ambivalenz* (Mainz: Von Zabern, 2003), esp. 243–270.

preached the Hutterite faith wherever they went, even in other Anabaptist communities, which led to several conflicts since this was considered "stealing the sheep."

The Hutterites of the 16th century practiced very strict church discipline, which included a two-fold application of the ban. With the Major Ban the guilty person was excommunicated; with the Minor Ban, the person in question had to live separately from the rest of the community. They ate alone at a table called "the table for those who have fallen away [*der abgefallenen tisch*]." Reacceptance into the community took place after sincere repentance with the laying on of hands by the elders.

To organize their communal life, the Hutterites appointed people to different positions; some of which have already been mentioned.[12] On the spiritual side, there were the ministers, also known as *Diener des Worts*, and on the economic side, the stewards, also known as *Diener der Notdurft*. An overseer presided over each of the work departments. Other positions ensured the caretaking of the community. The *Haushalter* presided over the individual duties [*Dienste*], over the kitchen and the cellar; he was also responsible for bookkeeping and administering the common treasury. The *Weinzierl* was responsible for work in the fields and in the vineyards, safekeeping and serving the wine, and keeping the barrels clean. Among other positions, the server [*Essentrager*] also gets mentioned. He was in charge of the kitchen and the dining hall [*Essenstube*], serving the members with food and drink and making sure things did not get too loud during the meals.

Among the women, the *Haushalterin* held the top position. She was called "mother of all sisters" and supervised the spinning and cotton operations. In addition, the *Haushalterin* presided over all female positions in the community. Among these was the "guardian of the kitchen [*Wächterin in der Kuchl*]," who was responsible for the care of the sick during the night and had to tend the fire and light, as well as the *Betterin*, who was in charge of the beds for the sick and for the school children.

---

12 See: "*Allgemeine Dienstordnung*," 1580, Cod. EAH 165, 33–50, Bruderhof Historical Archive, Walden, New York.

Hutterite society was, therefore, well organized and structured. The *Chronicle* describes it this way:

> Everyone, wherever he was, worked for the common good to supply the needs of all and to give help and support wherever it was needed. It was indeed a perfect body whose living, active members served one another.
>
> Think of the ingenious work of a clock, where one piece helps another to make it go, so that it serves its purpose. Or think of the bees, those useful little insects working together in their hive, some making wax, some honey, some fetching water, until their noble work of making sweet honey is done, not only for their own needs but enough to share with man. That is how it was among the brothers.
>
> So there has to be an order in all areas, for the matters of life can be properly maintained and furthered only where order reigns—even more so in the house of God, whose Master Builder and Establisher is the Lord himself. Where there is no order, there is disorder. There God does not dwell, and the house soon collapses.[13]

This quoted passage from the *große Geschichtsbuch* portrays the Hutterite community as an ideal society: nobody was idle, everybody participated and contributed to the wellbeing of the community. These passages are commonly interpreted as an actual "description" of the Hutterites, in which the community is compared to clockwork or to a beehive, in order to highlight its industriousness and its mechanical reliability—one cog meshed with the other and everything functioned together to make the common work and life possible. As fitting as these images are in describing a well-functioning and well-organized society, they remain ideal images. They reflect a desired ideal of what Hutterite society should look like. The *Gemeindeordnungen* demonstrate why this is the case.

---

13 *The Chronicle of the Hutterian Brethren*, vol. 1 (Rifton: Plough Publishing House, 1987), 406f.

The Hutterite *Gemeindeordnungen* (Community Ordinances)

A variety of *Gemeindeordnungen* ensured that the Hutterite communities functioned well.[14] They were essential in providing structure and order to Hutterite society; the size of their communities made rules and regulations necessary. The *Ordnungen* developed particularily after 1565—under the *Vorsteher* Peter Walpot, Hans Kräl, Klaus Braidl, and Sebastien Dietrich. They regulated how each member should conduct themselves and which tasks the different offices [*Ämter*] were responsible for. Thus, there were regulations for each different domains.

Ordnungen were developed for the social and interpersonal life, such as regulations for the service of the *Haushalter*, the *Haushalterin*, and those involved in attending to the daily needs of the members. Regulations in the *Kuchlordnung* specified the type of food every member or the different groups in the community should receive. For example, those who worked harder received richer food and larger portions. Detailed instructions were given on how pregnant women, the sick, and older people should be provided for, and which provisions were to be made available in difficult times.

Moreover, Hutterites produced *Ordnungen* for the different work departments [*Handwerke*]. They determined how a product was to be manufactured, how it should look, and which materials were to be used. Other *Ordnungen* spelled out which trades [*Handwerke*] should be involved in making a specific product. For example, the tailors, locksmiths, saddlers, blacksmiths and wagon-builders—all trades practiced on Hutterite *Bruderhöfe*—worked together in the production of carriages.

The *Ordnungen* are a fascinating type of source, as they enable a unique and diverse glimpse into the life of the Hutterites—into their social coexistence, into their spiritual meetings, and into their economic activities. But the *Ordnungen* also reveal what did not function so well in the community; in the course of the 16th century a number of problems arose that needed to be controlled and the *Ordnungen* convey these as well. When the same issue is ad-

---

14 von Schlachta, *Hutterische Konfession*, esp. 25–49, 111–132.

dressed repeatedly for several consecutive years, we can conclude that it was a persistent problem. Thus, the *Ordnungen* are a corrective to the sometimes-idealistic perspective of the *Geschichtsbuch*: the clock did not always run smoothly. The swarm of bees did not always fly tirelessly about; rather, some acted like drones. From this we can conclude that, although Hutterite life in the 16th century became increasingly well-organized, massive problems also developed in the lived experience of community life.

Individualism and its infiltration into *Gütergemeinschaft* were a recurring issue for Hutterites throughout their history. The struggle is revealed in a proverb from the 1560s: "[Obedience to] God's Word would not be so difficult, if only selfishness didn't exist. [*Gottes Wort wär nit so schwär, wenn nur der Aigen Nutz nit wär.*]" Individualism spelled death for an order based on the sharing of material things. There are countless examples of this in the Hutterite *Ordnungen*. We read of reports of craftsmen who lined their pockets and did not bring the earnings to the *Haushalter*. The sources also reveal how the craftsmen did this: they added an extra charge to the established price and pocketed the difference. The rest of the money was delivered to the *Haushalter*. Other craftsmen worked evenings and nights and sold the goods to benefit their private accounts.

The good and comfortable standard of living Hutterites experienced, at the latest by the middle of the 16th century, did not necessarily have a positive effect on their communal life.[15] A desire for personal belongings and lavish furnishings in sleeping quarters had been awakened. Due to popular demand, Hutterites often produced luxury items. The customers placed their orders and the Hutterites responded. Gradually, however, the demand for luxury items spread from the paying customers to community members. Increasingly, Hutterites began producing items such as expensive and ornately decorated pottery, beautifully crafted knives and elegant clothing for their own people. From the *Ordnungen* we know that late 16th century Hutterites were very well dressed; they wore expensive clothes and beautiful, colourful silks. The *Gemeindeordnungen* regularly call for members to dress themselves simply and decently, and to be mindful of their outward appearance. For ex-

---

15 von Schlachta, *Hutterische Konfession*, esp. 293–319.

ample, there was a rule that clothing should not be dyed. Also, the pottery made for use in the community should use plain colours and be glazed without elaborate patterns.

Moreover, the sources betray that some Hutterites lived a very extravagant life, which included the regular and copious consumption of alcohol. In 1610, for example, the millers and the farm overseers [*Meier*] are admonished to drink less wine. The concern was that one would smell it and those involved would "lose their reputation among the people or nobility and be considered reckless."[16] The *Abendmahl* also comes up regularly in the sources, indicating that too much alcohol was being consumed, turning the celebration into an orgy of overeating and drinking. An *Ordnung* from 1612 is especially bizarre: "When criminals are executed, our people should not run to watch."[17] Apparently, Hutterites had developed a taste for observing executions, which were considered a "must see" or spectacle in the Early Modern period; only a few decades earlier, the Hutterites were the ones being executed.

A further factor led to the undermining of *Gütergemeinschaft*: Hutterites began organizing their lives more individualistically. This is evident in the growing importance attributed to one's family. Life again focused more on the family, which in early times had played a subordinate role. Members planted their own gardens, in which they grew vegetables and raised small domestic animals and people increasingly retreated from communal life. Hutterites came less frequently to the common table [*Große Stube*], choosing instead to take their meals at home. Moreover, people left the community without permission to visit the neighbouring city, marketplace, or taverns.

In principle, there is nothing to say against a certain level of individuality, if it doesn't get out of hand, and doesn't destroy the common life, the fellowship—*das gemeinschaftliche Leben*. Communal life requires the maturity and responsibility of each person, but also rules that everybody observes. Still, it is important that these rules

---

16 Andreas Ehrenpreis, "*Auszug etlicher der Gemein Ordnungen* [Excerpts from several Community Ordinances]," transcript by Josef Beck, 113.
17 Karl and Franziska Peter, eds., *Der Gemein Ordnungen* [The Community Ordinances] *(1651-1873)* (Reardan, 1980), 50.

are repeatedly tested: Do they support the common life, or make it too rigid? In the Hutterite community of the late 16th century the 'good life,' individualism, the striving for personal gain, and the increasing importance of the family structures gradually undermined the principle of *Gütergemeinschaft*.

The *Gemeindeordnungen* give further insight into yet another interesting development, which was seen as a threat to the community. A hierarchical structure developed inside the community, so that not everybody was viewed or treated equally. Some Hutterites were "more equal" than others. Already from the beginning, the elders enjoyed "double honour," that is, they received better food and ate separately from the other members—there was a "table for the elders," sometimes even a special dining room. The *Kuchlordnungen* also reveal that, until the early 17th century, the *Ältesten* received richer and finer food; reports from outsiders reveal that the *Ältesten* dressed themselves more lavishly.

The principle of "double honour" was repeatedly criticized as hypocrisy and as undermining the very idea of *Gemeinschaft*. For example, at the beginning of the 1530s, Wilhelm Reublin, an Anabaptist from Württemberg who visited the Hutterites in Moravia, wrote that the *Ältesten* at Austerlitz "were leading lives like the nobility [*gleich den edeln ir leben fueren*]." They enjoyed meat, fish, and good wine, while the rest of the members had to be content with peas and cabbage. A different source from 1558 reports that "the leaders [of the Hutterite community] were dressed and ate in superior fashion [*die vorsteher (der Hutterischen Gemeinde) ir oberkait [seien], sic kleiden sich sonder und essen auch sonder*]."[18] A song from Johann Eysvogel also portrays Hutterites in a very unfavourable light, picking up on the luxury and special treatment of Hutterite leaders:

> They fatten the choicest cattle
> the best oxen, geese, pigs,
> and all manner of poultry.
> Everything must go to the Servants,
> whatever they wished and wanted,
> of fine food and drink

---
18   Packull, *Hutterite Beginnings*, esp. 215–219.

[is put] on the Servants' tables.
They ensnared attractive women—
take faithful heed of this.[19]

Even though there is a good deal of polemic in these descriptions, a kernel of truth can still be found in them. Within the Hutterite community itself the "double honour" treatment was increasingly viewed critically, as the *Gemeindeordnungen* from Andreas Ehrenpreis' era make clear. Ehrenpreis himself saw this practice as inappropriate and criticized leaders who elevated themselves by claiming too many privileges. Though the *Ordnungen* written by Andreas Ehrenpreis date from the middle of the 17th century, we can assume that he gathered and summarized existing *Ordnungen* relating to this matter. The practice of "double honour" was, therefore, likely already criticized at an earlier time.

Reasons for the Decline of the Hutterite Community in Moravia

The question arises: Why did these problems develop inside the Hutterite community? First of all, external conditions were responsible because they contributed to the prosperity Hutterites enjoyed. Secondly, the growth of the community, and thirdly, the inadequate integration of children—the next generation—also contributed to the decline.

The Conditions: Integration and Tolerance in Moravia

The tolerant atmosphere which reigned in Moravia in the second half of the 16th century, created a climate in which the community could prosper. The persecution ended and Hutterites were tolerated. On the basis of their economic output—the production of high-quality manufactured goods—they were even highly valued. Things went well for the community, difficulties were minimal, and Hutterites amassed considerable wealth. Noblemen from distant regions bought their products; Hutterite doctors were employed by burghers [*Bürger*] and the aristocracy. From the 1560s on, one

---

19 Hans Jedelhauser, *Zwelff wichtige vnd starcke Vrsachen* (Ingolstadt: Wolffgang Eder, 1587), fol. 36v: "*Das beste Vieh sie mösten / Von Ochssen Gänß und Schwein / Allerley Geflügl das beste / Muß alles in Dienern sein / Von Wilt und von Vischen / von kostbarlicher Speiß / Wol auff der Diener Tischen / schön Weiber zu ihn wischen / Das merckt mit gantzem fleiß.*"

speaks of the 'good' and then of the 'golden years:' no persecution, abundance, wealth and respectability. All of this is not only apparent from the crown glass windows [*Butzenfenstern*] in Hutterite dwellings, but also, for example, from the fact that meat regularly appeared on the menu. However, the 'good' and 'golden years' did not necessarily produce good Hutterites; the tolerant and well-to-do climate was a breeding ground for the neglect of the spiritual roots. The economic success became a dominant, determining influence for the community.

Growth of the Community and Integration of New-Comers

Because Hutterites were convinced that a Christian life based on their rules was only possible in Moravia, everyone who heard and accepted the preaching of the Hutterite missionaries and wanted to become Hutterite, had to migrate to Moravia. As a result, even in the second half of the 16th century, many new-comers arrived in Moravia to join the Hutterites. This influx of immigrants posed several challenges for the community, since all new-comers had to be integrated. In response, the Hutterites implemented special religious instruction which each new-comer had to attend.

In a 1607 letter to the chaplain at the imperial hospital in Vienna, the former Hutterite Lorentz Grötzner wrote that the new-comers were first sent to the *Vorsteher* of the church community, who divided them among the individual households. Here they were expected to take their time to study the Hutterite life and culture, "diligently attend to the Word of our Lord, and no longer think of the Egypt they left behind [*fleissig auf das Wort des Herrn merken, und nit mehr in Egypten hinter sich gedenken*]." Alongside the young Hutterites who had grown up in the community and finished school, they received spiritual instruction over several weeks. "After several weeks, the novices and also the older ones [*die Grossen*], who had been raised in their schools, listened to three sermons and were baptized, if they had earned a good report."[20] According to a report addressed to a Venetian judge in the early 1560s, novices were given "at least 8–14 days, and under special circumstances, a month, so that they could become well acquainted with the life

---

20   Ferdinand Menčik, "Ein Schreiben über die Wiedertäufer," in *Zeitschrift des deutschen Vereins für die Geschichte Mährens und Schlesiens*, 1911, 366.

and culture of the community, in order to make a sound decision about joining.[21]

Yet a further problem presented itself. Among the newcomers were not only people who were interested in the Hutterite faith, but some who came to Moravia because they had economic difficulties in their home territory. They hoped to find a 'good life,' or 'paradise on earth' on the economically prosperous Hutterite communities and could be called economic refugees. Thus, at the end of the 16th century, a high percentage of people on the Hutterite communities enjoyed the good life and prosperity but were not grounded in its spiritual foundation.[22]

Converts are a good thing for a community, since they keep a community vibrant and alive. They challenge the older members to answer the questions of the newer members. The newcomers question the old system because they have to get to know it, and the older members are challenged to find answers to their questions; that is, they have to engage their faith and life once again. This process keeps a community alive as members have to rediscover the purpose for living this way, bringing necessary renewal. But when the spiritual norms, which are fundamental to the Hutterite way, are no longer accepted by members of the community, this soon leads to bigger problems.

The Problem of the Next Generation

The children of the community—the next generation—posed a further difficulty. The Hutterites were unsuccessful at integrating their own children, at inspiring them to embrace the Hutterite faith to a satisfactory extent. It has been said that "faith cannot be inherited." To be an Anabaptist means to find an inner, personal 'yes' to the question of faith and to be baptized based on one's convictions. A *Lehr* on Colossians 2:16–23, possibly originating in the 17th century, puts it this way:

> And even if he were as old as Methuselah, and had a beard that touched the ground, and was raised in the community of God; his father might be the

---

21 Karl Benrath, "Wiedertäufer im Venetianischen um die Mitte des 16. Jahrhunderts." *Theologische Studien und Kritiken*, 58 (1885), 43.
22 von Schlachta, *Hutterische Konfession*, esp. 351–366.

most conscientious and distinguished person, yet he lives like the world, and abandons the command of Jesus Christ, is not a servant of Christ, but a servant of the world and its father [Satan].[23]

Faith and being Hutterite cannot be transferred to the children; rather it must be the result of a conscious decision.

How does one raise children to live as conscientious Hutterites, not only becasue they were born Hutterite, but because they have accepted and embraced the community and what it stands for? These are not only questions that we ask ourselves today; they were already important for Hutterites in the 16th century. These questions came to attention especially by mid-century. During the 'good' and 'golden years' children born in the community could not draw on experiences of persecution or confessional and political pressure, which had shaped the first generation, an experience which had produced a passionate, enduring faith. Rather, later generations were born into a community of prosperity.

What further complicated matters was that it must not have been easy for the emerging generation to leave the community. In the Early Modern period, the Hutterites lived in a foreign-language environment. The majority language in Moravia was Czech, and the German-speaking world was far away. Becoming a member of the community could thus easily become a mandatory event. A *Gemeindeordnung* of 1612 laments about this problem: "We see how many undisciplined children our schools produce, who become a burden [*mühselige Leute*] to the community, and even lose themselves in the world."[24]

Thus, the question is how to successfully pass on the fire of a freely chosen and authentic faith to the next generation. The historian Robert Friedmann spoke of the "fire of the first love" in the early generation of the Hutterites. Shaped by voluntariness [*Freiwilligkeit*] and maturity, the fire of "first love" ought to be passed on to the children. How was it passed on? And what was actually passed on? As a proverb reminds us: "Tradition is the passing on of the fire,

---

23 Hutterite Homily on Colossians 2:16–23, Paul S. Entz transcription, 1926, 198.
24 Andreas Ehrenpreis, "*Auszug etlicher der Gemein Ordnungen*," Josef Beck Abschrift, 66, 68.

not the veneration of the ashes." Ashes are thrown away. The fire is the living, burning reality; in the case of a religious community, it is above all the intellectual-spiritual and transcendent ideas. The spiritual idea behind Hutterite life—behind *Gütergemeinschaft*—is embodied through faith in Jesus Christ.

Hutterite Reactions to These Changes

Recording History

By the middle of the 16th century, the Hutterites began writing the history of their community. The intent was to preserve the past and the early years of the community for future generations—renewal through remembering! In the preface to *das Große Geschichtsbuch*, the Hutterite chronicler Kaspar Braitmichel observed,

> In my estimation, this record is a wonderful mirror in which every believer [*Gottglaubigen*] can see how he can protect himself from division, error, and anything that does not serve to honour God.[25]

Braitmichel retold or recorded the stories of the martyrs—the men and women who were "strong in faith"—from the early renewal movement.

Spiritual Writings

Many Hutterites in the 16th century recorded their thinking and ideas. Letters, confessions, and spiritual meditations were produced, which indicated the vitality of the community. Thinking about what it meant to be Hutterite was a common process in which many members participated. Being "Hutterite" was thus not a theoretical superstructure, dictated from above by the elders, but something that was internalized by the members, because they were actively thinking about these matters.

With the publication of Peter Riedemann's *Rechenschaft* in the 1540s, Hutterites received their foundational confession. Peter Walpot's *Artikelbuch*, which was written shortly thereafter, represents another of the essential writings that synthesized the Hutterite faith. Among other matters, it contained three important points

---

25 *Das große Geschicht-buch der Hutterischen Brüder*, XL. For an alternate translation see, *The Chronicle of the Hutterian Brethren*, vol. 1, LXXIV.

that were frequently discussed: baptism, the Lord's Supper, and *Gemeinschaft*. In addition, Hutterites began to write down their teachings [*Lehren*] and the letters written by missionaries who were active in the different regions across Germany were collected in bound volumes. Beyond this, texts focusing on *Gütergemeinschaft* also appeared.

Gemeindeordnungen

Initially, the elders responded by attempting to strengthen the spiritual life of the community. At the same time, they placed a great deal of emphasis on the *Gemeindeordnungen*. As has already been mentioned, these *Ordnungen* were important for a community like the Hutterites. They provided norms that made life in community possible. On the other hand, *Ordnungen* and traditions also have their pitfalls. They can have a negative effect on the community if they solidify and become rigid to the extent that the spiritual dimension is restricted, robbing the community of its inner spirit; orthodoxy is then primarily measured by how a member conforms to the external rules.

Opportunity for Reflection

To what extent was the external system of *Ordnungen* part of the Hutterite faith? What is the relationship between *Ordnungen* and faith today?

LECTURE TWO
"Test everything and hold fast to what is good."[1]

The Expulsion from Moravia and the Invitation to Transylvania

The saying, "It is only with good order that something can endure."[2] was vigorously put to the test among the Hutterites. Due to external political pressure and internal developments, the Hutterite community found itself in an increasingly difficult situation in the early 17th century. The winds of adversity were already assailing them by 1600. The economy remained robust, but it caused the community to be perceived as an overpowering competitor by the business community in South Moravia. According to the sources, there was concern that Hutterites were stealing the bread from the mouths of the other craftsmen by taking all the orders and buying up all the supplies. In order to prevent the competition from becoming even worse for the craftsmen in the cities, a resolution of the Diet in 1600 prohibited the establishment of new *Bruderhöfe*.

The political situation also became more severe as confessional politics intensified. Since the second half of the 16th century, the Habsburg rulers in Moravia had established a Jesuit mission with the aim of re-catholicizing the Protestant nobles, a mission which also targeted the Hutterites. Evidence for this mission include the polemical writings of Christoph Erhard and Christoph

---
1   1 Thessalonians 5:21.
2   Rudolf Wolkan, *Das große Geschichtbuch der Hutterischen Brüder* (Macleod/Wien, 1923), 335.

Andreas Fischer, which contained portrayals of Hutterite life on their covers. Although the Hutterites were protected by the nobles on whose estates they settled and in whose coffers they poured money, the Jesuit mission gradually made inroads. More and more nobles became Catholic, which increased the confessional tension and strengthened the influence of the Catholic Church and the Catholic Habsburg rulers in Moravia. This situation was playing itself out at the beginning of the Thirty Years' War (1618–1638).

After the Battle of the White Mountain in November 1620, all Protestants and Anabaptists in the Habsburg territories faced severe repression. Mind you, these measures were not only directed against Hutterites, but affected all non-Catholic groups since a general policy of Recatholicization was in effect. In Moravia, the situation was particularly severe because the Bohemian nobles had revolted against the emperor at the beginning of the Thirty Years' War.

In 1622, the landlords on whose estates the Hutterites had settled received an imperial order from Vienna to expel their tenants from Moravia within four weeks. Many of the nobles attempted to protect the Hutterites to the very end, because they did not want to sacrifice their labour force and their products. Many nobles patronized the Hutterites even after the expulsion and some secretly brought craftsmen back again. According to the figures, approximately 10,000 left, which was about one-third of the total Hutterite population.[3]

The rest of the Hutterites remained in Moravia or Upper Hungary, where already in the 16th century a second area with Hutterite *Haushaben* had developed. Among these were Velke Levare (also known as Lewär or Großschützen) and Sabatisch, both of which are found in Slovakia today. Thus, two-thirds of the Hutterites did not leave Moravia, but stayed behind and either converted to Catholicism or continued to live as Hutterites on the *Höfe* in Upper Hungary.

The *Chronicle* reports that,

> The Lord had sent this distress to his people as

---

3   Winkelbauer, *Die Vertreibung der Hutterer*, 73f.

The home of Joseph Hörndel, the potter, at Lewär (Velke Levare). [SOURCE: Jan Glaysteen.]

a test and purification to reveal the proven ones. Many could not stand the test, particularly the superficial and insincere, even though they had left Moravia. They were just like the children of Israel, who left Egypt, but as soon as they were faced with suffering, disaster, hunger, and cold, thought about Egypt (where they had had bread in plenty) and turned back, abandoning the Lord and his church. Many did not even leave the country but left the church in Moravia (most of these being people from the cardinal's estates).[4]

Thus, the expulsion from Moravia demonstrates that there must have been many Hutterites who lacked an inner connection to the

---

4   *Chronicle*, vol. 1, 675.

community and a depth of spiritual conviction, and who therefore were not willing to set out for a new home. But the expelled Hutterites did not go in complete uncertainty, for even before the expulsion some had received an offer of settlement. The Transylvanian prince Gábor Bethlen had invited them in order to bolster the economy in his territories with the quality craftsmanship and the reliable workmanship of the Hutterites. Bethlen extended favourable conditions and granted the community extensive privileges.[5]

The settlement policy enacted by Bethlen—from which many persecuted subjects, including Hutterites, benefited—was typical of the Early Modern era: a prince or lord invited new subjects, including those who were persecuted because of their faith but recognized for their innovative and good work, in order to strengthen his own territory. This policy worked in the Hutterites' favour at the beginning of the 17th century. Similarly, in the 18th century, Mennonites were often invited to settle a region because they were known for their innovative agricultural methods. In this way, persecuted 'heretics' became welcomed subjects. Policies like this were seldom motivated by altruism, but rather by economic interests, which was also true of the settlement of the Hutterites in Moravia in the early 16th century.

Close to 2000 Hutterites who were driven out of Moravia went to Transylvania; the rest continued to live or settled anew in Upper Hungary. In the 17th century, therefore, Hutterites were settled in two regions: Upper Hungary and Transylvania. The regions were very distant from each other, which presented challenges for the administration of the larger community.

The Success and Decline of the Hutterite Community in the 17th Century

First, a glimpse at the development of the community itself. In the first half of the 17th century, the Hutterites continued to be very strong economically and were able to maintain their good reputation. Sources report that "Hutterite tanners and tawers did a superior job of processing hides than the local tanners" and their

---

5   von Schlachta, *From the Tyrol to North America*, esp. 73–79.

carriage makers [*Kutschenmacher*] produced better scythes than the local craftsmen.[6] It was the workmanship of Hutterite hatmakers, tailors, cobblers, waggoners, blacksmiths, locksmiths and knife makers that contributed most to the community's outstanding reputation. Hutterite ceramics also continued to be in high demand and stove fitters did not just manufacture tableware, but installed tiled stoves in countless aristocratic castles and residences as well. Hutterite tiled stoves typically featured white tin glaze or blue cobalt glaze with plants and ornamental flowers or a green lead glaze. It is also documented that Hutterites in Transylvania practiced agriculture. Fruit, meadow, and acreage farming, as well as sheep shearing are mentioned in the sources. Clearly, the Hutterites brought the 'Moravian sheep' or the proverbial golden goose to Transylvania. Like in Moravia, Hutterite barber-surgeons were employed by the nobility.

Hans Jakob Christoffel von Grimmelshausen provides a very intriguing description of 17th century Hutterites in the 19th chapter of book five of his 1669 work, *Simplicissimus*:

> In the first place they had plenty of treasure and more than enough to eat. However, they wasted none of it, nor did a single curse or murmur of displeasure leave their lips. I never heard a superfluous word uttered among them. I saw only craftspeople working away as if earning their livelihoods. In schools, teachers instructed not classes of youngsters but so many adorable children—quite as if they had been their own. Nowhere did I see menfolk and womenfolk bundled in together. The sexes occupied separate premises, each separately performing their appointed tasks. [...] Elsewhere I saw females doing nothing but spin, in rooms that might contain up to a hundred wheels. Or one might do the laundry, another make beds, a third see to the animals, a fourth wash the dishes, a fifth wait at table, a sixth be in charge of table linen. Of

---

6   Magdalena Bunta, "Die Habaner in Siebenbürgen," *Keramos* 104 (1984): 79–85, esp. 81.

> the others, too, each knew what to do. And just as the various jobs were neatly distributed among the womenfolk, each man and boy had his particular function. If one person (male or female) fell ill, he or she was assigned a personal medical attendant as well as a general doctor and apothecary of the appropriate sex. In fact, though, so good was their diet and so excellently ordered their existence that they seldom did fall ill. I saw many a fine figure hopping about in the best of health at a ripe old age, which was something not often seen elsewhere. [...] Of anger there was no sign, nor was there of agitation, animosity, jealousy, hostility, care for secular interests, arrogance, or any regret. In sum, all was loving harmony, every one's sole concern (apparently) that of increasing the human race and extending the kingdom of God in all modesty and respectability.[7]

Grimmelshausen's description fits with the quotation from the "description of the community" in das *Große Geschichtsbuch*—a picture of an almost perfectly organized society. It is not known which *Hof* Grimmelshausen described, and it is not even clear whether he personally visited a *Hof* or simply reported what he had heard. However, we can infer from this quotation that Hutterite society was viewed positively by outsiders, which is extremely interesting and noteworthy. When Grimmelshausen's portrayal is examined more closely, placed in its proper context and viewed against the background of the general situation within Hutterite society, this much must be said: Grimmelshausen presents a somewhat idyllic picture, which fits his intention of writing an adventure and coming-of-age novel [*Entwicklungsroman*]. His protagonist, the rascal or fool Simplicius Simplicissimus, was always on the hunt for a good and successful life, for the perfect society. Thus, the author introduces his readers to several examples, including the Hutterites.

Wherever and through whom Grimmelshausen encountered the Hutterites, the community he described must have been one from

---

7   Hans Jakob Christoffel von Grimmelshausen, *The Adventures of Simplicius Simplicissimus*, J.A. Underwood, trans. (London: Penguin Books, 2018), 141–142.

the first half of the 17th century. For only during the founding years in Transylvania did the community fare well. Even then, not everything ran smoothly. Drawing on the *Gemeindeordnungen* of that time as a comparative source, it becomes clear that the Hutterites in Transylvania brought their problems from Moravia along with them. Once again, community discipline left something to be desired. The prosperity which continued at first in Transylvania again led to idleness and to disregard for the *Ordnungen*. Thus, the "lovely harmony" described by Grimmelshausen is revealed to be a utopia.

In addition, the distance between Upper Hungary and Transylvania proved to be too great for effective administration of the entire Hutterite movement.[8] Although good contacts existed between both regions, there were visits in both directions, and mutual assistance was exchanged during times of need, the two groups developed in different directions. It was difficult to enforce common norms across such a great distance in the 17th century because communication and ensuring compliance was logistically difficult.

For an assessment of the situation in the Hutterite communities of the 17th century we can look to the words of Andreas Ehrenpreis, one of the most well-known *Ältesten* of this period (1639–1662). He lamented repeatedly that individualism and private property and a rather lax spiritual life had taken hold in the community—familiar words, when one remembers the complaints of the late 16th century. In two appeals and admonitions [*Bitt- und Vermahnungsschreiben*] from the years 1642 and 1649 addressed to the communities in Alwinz and Bodtok, Ehrenpreis criticized the fact that the offices [*Dienste*] in the community were not being conscientiously exercised according to the guidelines found in the *Ordnungen*. Members of the community had ceased to fear God. Parents and schoolmasters failed to set a good example for their children. Members disregarded the ministry and the Servants of the Word, ridiculing and talking disparagingly about them. The Hutterites had "grown lax and disinterested in appreciating and

---

8   Wes Harrison, *Andreas Ehrenpreis and Hutterite Faith and Practice* (Kitchener: Pandora Pres, 1997), 41–48; von Schlachta, *From the Tyrol to North America*, 79–81.

being concerned about their salvation [*urdrüssig und satt an dem Schatz ihres Heils und an dem Dienst ihrer Seligkeit*]."⁹

Some community members also expressed their dissatisfaction about the direction the Hutterites were taking. From time to time people voiced their concerns, criticizing the spiritual orientation of the community and above all, calling for a more serious faith commitment, and demanding more devotion rather than merely following external rules. For example, in 1629 Benjamin Kengel from Sabatisch criticized the fact that too much emphasis was being put on rules and ceremonies and the Holy Spirit was not adequately heeded. Kengel followed his concern with action, staying away from communal worship because he thought it was a "human tradition and not inspired by the Holy Spirit." He criticized the celebration of the Lord's Supper as merely "outward customs and ceremonies and *Ordnungen*," which "were not necessary for a true Christian." Baptism and church offices were likewise regarded as human traditions. His criticisms picked up on the central place that ceremonies and rituals had taken in the community's life.[10] Later, in the 18th century, there were also regular demands from Hutterites for a more flexible spiritual life and to consider which customs were actually necessary and where changes were needed. Even though such demands were often met with criticism from community leaders, they are evidence of a vibrant community.

Andreas Ehrenpreis' statements and the criticisms of other members of the community point to the following conclusion: Until the middle of the 17th century there were many 'cultural Hutterites' in the community, that is, members who valued the good life and were 'Hutterite' in name, but were not committed to the spiritual foundations and norms of the community. In sociological-religious terms: a Hutterite 'community' [*Gemeinschaft*] of voluntary members convicted inwardly by faith and a life together became a 'church' [*Kirche*]. A typical characteristic of a church is that a certain percentage of members do not really participate in the life of the community and rarely or never attend worship. This is not a problem most churches seriously contend with because less

---

9   *Chronicle*, vol. 1, 737–743, 752–760.
10 von Schlachta, *From the Tyrol to North America*, 101f.

dedicated members simply continue to be counted as members. For the Hutterites, however, this situation had a significant impact because the spiritual, social, and economic aspects of life were more closely intertwined. Those who were less committed still practiced *Gütergemeinschaft*; they worked and participated to some extent in the life of the community, but an essential element of their life in community was missing—namely, the spiritual basis and the conscious responsibility toward God. In this way, several factors acted like 'sand in the machine' of *Gütergemeinschaft*.

The Hutterites Within the Anabaptist World

It has already been mentioned that Anabaptism of the 16th century was a diverse and vibrant movement. All Anabaptists agreed that infant baptism was unbiblical and that only mature adult believers should be baptized based on a personal confession of faith, but there was debate about many other topics. An essential point of contention was the Anabaptist position regarding politics, which included questions about non-resistance, swearing of oaths, and occupying political office. There were also debates about divorce, the Trinity, whether Jesus Christ had a human or a divine nature, and community-of-goods. The various Anabaptist groups in the 16th century, including the Hutterites, engaged in passionate arguments, often with a polemical edge. It is worth mentioning that in general, the 16th century was a century of polemic, and the Anabaptists were children of their time.

As polemical and passionate as these debates were, they bear witness to the fact that the Anabaptists had a mature expression of their faith; they were familiar with the convictions of other communities, reflected on their own convictions, and felt obliged to defend their position in both long and short works. In the 17th century the various Anabaptists groups continued to participate in lively discussions, as Andreas Ehrenpreis' *Sendbrief* shows in which he clarifies his positions in relation to current topics. For example, he devotes a chapter to the nature of Jesus Christ and whether he had a divine or human nature, or both. He thus entered a debate being conducted with Arians or Antitrinitarians, who denied the Trinity and were convinced that Jesus was merely human, and did not have a divine nature.

Another important topic in the *Sendbrief* is *Gütergemeinschaft*, which Ehrenpreis vigorously defends. He challenges his brothers and sisters to live it earnestly and to be stronger advocates for a life of intentional community and fellowship [*das gemeinschaftliche Leben*] in order to revive the missionary activity, which the Hutterites had so actively been engaged in during the 16th century. Now, in the middle of the 17th century, these activities had mostly come to an end, which Ehrenpreis blamed on the period of prolonged war. Yet the Hutterite *Ältester* strove to once again make Hutterite life attractive to outsiders. To his plea Ehrenpreis added a report on the uniting of various Swiss Brethren communities from the Palatinate with the Hutterites.[11] They had come to Moravia and joined the Hutterites in the second half of the 16th century. This report not only indicates the success of Hutterite mission work, but also reveals the arguments that developed about the question of *Gütergemeinschaft* in the 16th century because other Anabaptist groups felt censured by the Hutterite position that a Christian life was only possible in *Gütergemeinschaft*.

One must continually reflect upon the question: what role did *Gütergemeinschaft* play in the worldview [*Ideengebäude*] of the Hutterite community and how essential did they think it was and is for salvation? Many Hutterite texts, including several from Andreas Ehrenpreis, reveal a certain ambivalence about the answer to this question.[12] Ehrenpreis writes that on the one hand many people will speak and write against community-of-goods, "that *Gemeinschaft* and living together is not necessary." He tries to refute these views by referring to the fact that "whole clouds of witnesses stand in front of our eyes and bear witness (Heb. 12) that these articles are a sure sign by which one could recognize a true people of God." Thus, for Ehrenpreis, only a people that practice *Gütergemeinschaft* are a "true people of God." Moreover, he points out that "the frequently mentioned *Gemeinschaft*, as an expression of divine justice and righteousness, was expected of all who considered themselves Christian."[13]

11 Andreas Ehrenpreis, *Ein Sendbrief an alle diejenigen so sich rühmen [...] dass sie ein abgesondertes Volk von der Welt sein wollen [...]* (1652, Reprint: Scottdale, 1920), 155–189.
12 von Schlachta, *Hutterische Konfession*, 179–220.
13 Ehrenpreis, *Sendbrief*, 13f, 16, 19.

Yet, on the other hand, Ehrenpreis qualifies these statements by declaring that *Gemeinschaft* was not "absolutely essential for salvation." However, he added that it helped to reduce and focus the Christian life on what was necessary. "Authentic love" could only be practiced in *Gemeinschaft*—through love in word and deed. Where *Gemeinschaft* was not observed, "only a lifeless brotherhood and an inauthentic love in words alone" existed. Therefore, Ehrenpreis called for renewed mission work, in order to gather all believers under the roof of *Gütergemeinschaft*. The Hutterite *Ältester* defended his community against all accusations that Hutterites were using "violence and coercion" in their pursuit of *Gütergemeinschaft*. Nobody was to be forced; rather, he insisted that "whoever is not convicted by love, understanding and the Spirit of God, should not bother with it."[14]

Another interesting point can be inferred from the writings of Andreas Ehrenpreis, namely his openness to contacts with other confessional groups and his willingness to engage with the ideas of other communities and confessions. The Hutterite *Ältester* was familiar with the literature of his time. For example, he was familiar with the works of Johann Arndt and Johannes Piscator, two 17th century Protestant authors.

The Decline of the Hutterites in Transylvania

During the course of the 17th century the external pressure on the Hutterites grew, not least because of the Thirty Years' War and the Turkish Wars. *Bruderhöfe* were attacked, members were captured, and many were led away to be sold as slaves. The most familiar story involves Salomon Böger, a Hutterite miller, who pursued captured Hutterites as far as Constantinople at the beginning of the 17th century.[15] He was able to pay for the release of several people from prison and slavery, but for his efforts he landed in serious difficulties and conflict with the community's leaders. Böger began his journeys on his own initiative, because he wanted to rescue his own family, a decision that was sharply criticized by the elders. It was only some time later that the *Ältesten* supported Böger. In addition to the the various wars, recurring plagues tested the Hutterites.

---

14   Ehrenpreis, *Sendbrief*, 122–124.
15   von Schlachta, *Hutterische Konfession*, 266, 296.

By the second half of the 17th century at the latest, Hutterites completely ceased their missionary work. A final attempt was the establishment of a *Bruderhof* in Mannheim in the 1660s and 70s.[16] It had to be abandoned, however, due to the majority of its inhabitants joined the Reformed Church. The external pressure on the Hutterites was considerable. Tribulation and hardship were commonplace, along with internal controversies.

An especially tragic story shook the community of Alwinz in the 1690s. Georg Geissy, an Arian and Hutterite convert, quickly rose to a leadership position, becoming a teacher and elder in the community.[17] However, he left the community soon thereafter, taking a great portion of the community's wealth. The *Klein-Geschichtsbuch* reports that Geissy took "six or seven wagons of their prized possessions"—a catastrophic loss for the community.[18]

Over all, the developments described thus far had two effects. First, the number of Hutterites was substantially decimated. By 1738, the community in Alwinz had only 36 souls remaining. A letter written by Hutterites to Mennonites in Amsterdam provides the following numbers for the year 1748: the community in Sabatisch consisted of 38 couples, Lewär and Alwinz had 17 couples, St. Johann 11 couples, and Trentschin 4 couples. Second, the foundations of Hutterite faith fell into severe and prolonged instability, because the community gave up *Gütergemeinschaft*. In Transylvania this occurred in 1707 and it appears that the events surrounding Georg Geissy and his departure were a decisive factor, as the community was not able to recover economically. In Upper Hungary *Gütergemeinschaft* was abandoned at the latest by 1694; unfortunately, the exact dates are not known. *Ältester* Johannes Waldner reports about these events with the benefit of hindsight, mentioning

---

16   von Schlachta, *From the Tyrol to North America*, 81–83.
17   As already mentioned, the Arians or Antitrinitarians rejected the doctrines of the Trinity and the two natures of Christ; that is, they believed that Jesus Christ merely had a human nature and was subordinate to God the Father. We know of several Antitrinitarians that joined the Hutterites in the 17th century. Moreover, there were regular discussions between both groups, reflected by letter correspondence and by a visit of the Antitrinitarian scholar, Daniel Zwicker, to Sabatisch.
18   *Chronicle*, vol. 2, 316f.

repeatedly that the Hutterites now began living in private property. He doesn't, however, give an exact date when this occured.[19]

The Hutterite community was thus numerically devastated and had given up essential, foundational aspects of its faith. It is always difficult to write a "What would have happened if…" story, yet one can probably say this: If the Crypto-Protestants from Carinthia had not arrived, the Hutterites would have disappeared entierly.

The Connection with the Carinthian Crypto-Protestants

Political developments in Austria came to the aid of the devitalized Hutterites. Like in Moravia, and in the Bohemian lands more broadly, Protestants in other parts of the Habsburg territories came under pressure during the 1620s. They were required to leave the empire's territories, which many did not do, choosing instead to live their faith in secret. Publicly, they lived like Catholics; privately, they remained Protestant. These Protestants are called 'Secret' or 'Crypto-Protestants.'[20] Yet in their villages they often did not live very "secretly," because the inhabitants knew very well that there were Protestants among them and they mostly got along well with one another. Interestingly, the government also left the Crypto-Protestants alone for a long time.

By the late 17th century pressure against the Crypto-Protestants was growing and in the 18th century a new wave of persecution began. Many now had to leave their native land, especially in the regions of Carinthia, Steiermark, and Salzburg, and were deported to Transylvania, often under inhumane condition. Among them was a group of Crypto-Protestants from Carinthia, who were exiled to the eastern Habsburg territories in 1755. The deportees arrived and looked for work, which they were able to find on a Hutterite *Hof* in Alwinz. They learned about the life and faith of the Hutterites and after a time were so convinced by what they experienced that they joined the community and were baptized. These Protest-

---

19 von Schlachta, *From the Tyrol to North America*, esp. 85–88.
20 Rudolf Leeb, Martin Scheutz, and Dietmar Weikl, eds., *Geheimprotestantismus und evangelische Kirchen in der Habsburgermonarchie und im Erzstift Salzburg, 17./18. Jahrhundert* (Vienna: Böhlau/Munich: Oldenbourg, 2009).

ants brought 'fresh blood' to the Hutterites and were instrumental for the revival of the Hutterite faith and community.[21]

The Spiritual Life of the Hutterites

The joining of the Carinthian Protestants not only ensured the survival of the Hutterites, but also brought spiritual renewal. Although the life of the Hutterites continued to be oriented around the old *Ordnungen* and based on the writings of their ancestors, certain nuances are evident. There was a new openness to enter debates about other confessional directions and to integrate impulses from these exchanges. In the second half of the 18th century, this led to ongoing discussion about how to best shape and nurture the spiritual life of the community. However, one cannot draw the conclusion that the 'old' Hutterites with their origins in Anabaptism stood on one side, and the 'new' Hutterites, who originated out of a Pietist-oriented Protestantism, were on the other side. Or that the 'old' Hutterites were the rationalists and the 'new' Hutterites the modernizers or the 'spiritual ones.' This was not the case, and the participating groups reorganized themselves more organically, based on the issue at hand, as the various discussions unfolded.

Within Anabaptist scholarship the question has been posed about how big the theological differences between Anabaptists and Protestants really were, for example questions relating to soteriology, grace and works. This question is often answered in the direction that the difference was great, that the Anabaptists focused on following Jesus Christ or discipleship, while the Protestants relied on the grace of God and their faith was not evident in their everyday lives. In fact, the 16th century Anabaptists accused the Protestants in exactly this way. For their part, the Protestants assumed that Anabaptists disregarded grace and strove for works-righteousness.[22]

---

21 Erich Buchinger, "Die Geschichte der Kärntner Hutterischen Brüder in Siebenbürgen und in der Walachei (1755–1770), in Rußland und Amerika," Sonderdruck aus *Carinthia* 172 (1982), 145–303.

22 Robert Friedmann, *Mennonite Piety Through the Centuries: Its Genius and its Literature* (Goshen: Mennonite Historical Society, 1949/Eugene: Wipf and Stock, 1999); Astrid von Schlachta, "Anabaptists and Pietists: Influences, Contacts, and Relations," in Douglas H. Shantz, ed., *A Companion to German Pietism 1660–1800* (Leiden/Boston: Brill, 2015), 116–138, esp. 118–122; von Schlachta, *Täufer*, 119–124.

When one places these mutual accusations in the context of the 16th century, they appear to be a part of a polemical debate, which served the purpose of denigrating the other side and create distance from them. When one looks instead to the theological statements and texts of the different Anabaptist and Protestant authors, it becomes clear that the grace of God was also essential for Anabaptists. And Luther knew just as well as the Anabaptists that God's grace simply represents the beginning of a Christian life and that a Christian life must find its practical expression through works—in a life of discipleship.

Thus, the lines of the conflicts that presented themselves between the 'old' and 'new' Hutterites shortly after the Carinthian Crypto-Protestants joined the Hutterites did not follow typical theological issues such as grace or soteriology, but had to do with spiritual practices, for example, the method, form, or frequency of prayer. Other debates revolved around concrete matters, such as the marriage practices of the Hutterites. The new Hutterites opposed the old Hutterite practice of arranged marriages mediated by the *Ältesten*. Another controversy was about the intensity of work on Hutterite *Höfen*, or the relationship between work and spiritual life. Matthias Hofer, one of the new Carinthian Hutterites, was at the centre of many of these discussions. The *Klein-Geschichtsbuch* describes him as a man of prayer who was as familiar with the whole Bible as he was with the Lord's prayer. It is said he knew all the references in the Old and New Testament that pertained to prayer by heart. In addition, he composed many spiritual writings and became an important advisor to *Ältester* Hänsel Kleinsasser.

Matthias Hofer introduced a special prayer practice within the Hutterite community, based on Psalm 119, where it says: "At midnight I rise to praise you." He also referred to Psalm 134: "Come, bless the Lord, all you servants of the LORD, who stand by night in the house of the LORD!" Hofer introduced a custom in the community, where all members were woken at midnight for prayer. Actually, members were supposed to gather to pray together, but according to the *Klein-Geschichtsbuch* this was deemed improper and therefore each person prayed in bed—somebody led the prayer and the others prayed along. This practice of midnight prayer was maintained for several years. Yet Matthias Hofer provoked further debates, such as whether one should pray publicly and loud or quietly in one's private chamber. Interestingly, Mennonites were involved in the very same discussion during the 18th century.[23]

Matthias Hofer was one of the brothers who had been imprisoned in Hermannstadt during the 1750s because they resisted the catholicizing measures introduced by the Jesuits. This is where the debate was sparked, whether auidible or quiet prayer was right. Hofer was of the opinion that quiet prayer was of the devil, for to refuse to raise one's voice in prayer meant to worship the mute gods, or to be like a dog who could not bark. In addition, he was convinced quiet prayer was merely the prayer of hypocrites. To support his arguments, he found Bible passages that emphasized his points. According to Hofer, prayer should be "public before God." One should pray with others, "giving one another a helping hand according to the inner working of the Spirit." For Matthias Hofer, prayer was an expression of fellowship and therefore should be done out loud.

Moreover, Hofer was of the opinion that one should not sing while working; one should either work or sing. When one sings, said Hofer, one should stop working. Overall, he maintained that there was an inappropriate relationship between work and spiritual life among the Hutterites. And the Carinthian Hutterite had further ideas about how faith should be expressed. He thought that one should not remove one's hat to greet government officials or even not greet them at all. In addition, one should not work for "unbelievers." Already in the 16th century Hutterites had discussed whether one should work for Catholic lords or clerics. Behind this concern was the question of how intensive the contact with members of the Catholic church should be. How did Hutterites resolve the conflict about how to pray? They looked at the old community writings and discovered that the old *Ordnungen* specified that one should pray quietly. God also hears quiet prayers, it was written. Interestingly, Peter Riedemann dedicates a whole chapter to prayer in his *Rechenschaft*.[24] He doesn't address the question of how to

---

23 See the story of Matthias Hofer: *Chronicle*, vol. 2, 495–500.
24 Peter Riedemann, *Rechenschaft*, 120–122.

pray, but simply maintains that one should pray with a devoted heart and in faith. A little later, Matthias Hofer was so disappointed that he left the community and went to West Prussia where he established contact with Mennonites.

In general, it appears Hutterites in the late 18th century gathered quite frequently for worship or prayer. From the time of Hänsel Kleinsasser, who was *Ältester* from 1762 to 1779, the following worship order has been documented: members gathered to pray mornings, evenings and during mid-day. During the morning and mid-day meetings a spiritual text was read aloud. In addition, they met before breakfast and before supper and greeted each other with the sign of peace. In other words, the brothers embraced each other and the sisters embraced their fellow sisters. Brothers and sisters did not embrace but exchanged a handshake as a sign of peace. The Psalms from the Bible were prayed, from the first to the last. When the entire psalter had been prayed, they started again at the beginning. Following the prayer, two chapters were read from the Bible or another book and they concluded with singing. Perhaps this very extensive spiritual program reflects the zeal of the Carinthian newcomers.[25] After the death of Hänsel Kleinsasser the Hutterites discontinued the praying of Psalms and the communal morning prayer—now the community only gathered evenings. The *Klein-Geschichtsbuch* speaks of the following years as marked by a decline in the observance of the *Ordnungen*.

Hutterite Contacts with the Moravian Brethren

The Carinthian Crypto-Protestants were not the only connection the Hutterites had to the Protestant world in the 18th century. They also maintained regular contact with the Moravian Brethren, which allows interesting glimpses into the religious life of the Hutterites. The Moravian Brethren are closely associated with the name of the Saxon Count Nikolaus von Zinzendorf, who established a faith community in several villages west of Görlitz that welcomed many religious refugees in the early 18th century. In this way, many persecuted Bohemian Brethren from Moravia and Bohemia, whose

---

25 *Chronicle*, vol. 2, 499f, Heinrich Donner, "Kurzer Bericht von den Taufgesinnten Christen, welche die Hutterische Brüder genannt werden," *Gemeindeblatt für Mennoniten* 7, No. 6, (1876): 44f; No. 7: 53f; No. 8: 60–62.

origins can be traced to the Hussites of the 15th century, came to Saxony. Zinzendorf offered them refuge on his estates, thereby laying the foundation for the Moravian Brethren.[26]

Nikolaus von Zinzendorf and his communities [*Brüdergemeine*] were Pietists, a renewal movement that shaped Protestant churches since the 17th century.[27] In the 18th century Pietism also provided Anabaptist groups—several Mennonite congregations, but also among the Hutterites—with an essential impulse for renewal. The origins of Pietism can be traced to the Lutheran theologian Philipp Jacob Spener and his important work, *Pia Desideria*, which appeared in 1675. In this book he called for a more intensive internalized piety and a deepening of faith—all demands that kept appearing among Hutterites, as we have seen with Benjamin Kengel and Matthias Hofer. For Pietist thinkers, personal edification was as central to the believer's life as discussions regarding spiritual questions. To support this development, Philipp Jacob Spener suggested the formation of *collegia pietatis*. This involved organizing meetings for the purpose of nurturing faith [*Erbauungsversammlungen*], almost like the 'reading circles' found among the early Anabaptists. People gathered to read the Bible and pray together. Moreover, Pietism is characterized by a considerable openness toward other faith communities; on the basis of faith in Jesus Christ, one belonged to the community of all believers.

Thus, the piety of the Moravian Brethren aimed at a very internalized faith-life, for which the maturity of the believer was as central as the personal relationship to God. In addition, the Moravians were shaped by the desire for *Gemeinschaft*. Although they did not live in *Gütergemeinschaft* like the Hutterites, they administered a comparably comprehensive communal organization and lived and worked together very closely. This caught the attention of the Hutterites.

During the course of the 18th century there were regular contacts between the Hutterites and the Moravian Brethren, although the intensity of the contacts varied over time; at times, there was no

---

26 Dietrich Meyer, *Zinzendorf und die Herrnhuter Brüdergemeine 1700–2000* (Göttingen: Vandenhoeck & Ruprecht, 2000).
27 Johannes Wallmann, *Der Pietismus* (Göttingen: Vandenhoeck & Ruprecht, 2005).

contact at all, but the exchange reawakened several times. For their part, the Hutterites were motivated to maintain the relationship by the desire to find like-minded faith communities during a time of increasing persecution. They desired to be strengthened in their faith and to experience encouragement and edification through fellowship with others.

Very illustrative is a minor incident that led to the renewal of contact with the Moravian Brethren in the 1770s, after the relationship had been dormant for some time. The Moravians operated a settlement in Sarepta, which today is part of Wolgograd.[28] The contact came about after an officer who visited the Hutterites informed them that a Christian community lived "according to a spirit and order of the early apostolic church" in the Russian Gouvernement of Astrachan.[29] The Hutterites were intrigued and wanted to know more. Thus, the *Ältester* Hans Kleinsasser wrote a letter to the Moravian minister in Sarepta to enquire how important *Gemeinschaft* was for the Brethren—whether they "were a true *gemeinschaftliche* church or not." Though the Moravians responded, not much came of this initial exchange.

The relationship only intensified around 1800 and resulted in a very regular exchange, which was not limited to letter writing, but also included an interest in becoming familiar with the piety and foundational principles of the respective communities. Community texts and confessions of faith were exchanged and both groups shared about their successes and problems. For example, a document from the Moravians following a visit to the Hutterites reports that the Hutterite *Ältesten* had complained about the poor quality of candidates for the ministry and about the isolated state of the community. For that reason, according to this summary, the Hutterites were willing to unite with the Moravians. The Hutterite

---

28 Christlieb Suter, *Geschichte der Gemeine Sarepta 1765–1775*, Otto Teigeler, ed. (Herrnhut: Herrnhuter Verlag, 2003); J. Th. Müller, "Berührungen der alten und neuen Brüderunität mit den Täufern," *Zeitschrift für Brüdergeschichte*, vol. 4, (Herrnhut: Verlag des Vereins für Brüdergeschichte, 1910), 180–234; Astrid von Schlachta, "'Mit Religions Streitigkeiten wollen wir uns nicht befassen:' Begriffe und Konzepte im herrnhutisch-hutterischen Verhältnis," *Mennonitische Geschichtsblätter* 62 (2005): 51–76.

29 Regarding the relations between Hutterites and Herrnhuters, see: von Schlachta, "Mit Religions Streitigkeiten," 57–59.

Ältester Johannes Waldner was attracted by the "older and closer relation with the Moravian Brethren." In contrast, he had vehemently rejected an association with Mennonites.[30]

Although they never joined the Moravian Brethren, the Hutterites under Johannes Waldner appear to have engaged intensively with the ideas of the Herrnhuter. It is said that Johannes Waldner read the *Idea Fidei Fratrum*, a book by Moravian August Gottlieb Spangenberg, as well as other Moravian writings "with complete approval." He valued the Moravian Brethren's "Community Reports" and praised their pastors' conferences as a "good and very useful institution." In a letter to his Moravian correspondent Johann Wiegand, Johannes Waldner wrote that he was impressed by the Moravians' practice to encourage their members to read the Bible for themselves, something that Waldner thought "was held in contempt in so-called Christendom."[31]

Johannes Waldner also appears to have admired the Moravian practice of drawing lots to make decisions in the community. He described an instance where he intended to send some 16th century Hutterite texts to the Moravian Brethren. However, he had reservations about the very harsh polemics they contained, fearing that they might hurt the relationship with the Moravians. Waldner finally decided to resolve the question by lot—and so determined he should send the texts.

Additionally, Johannes Waldner's language reveals Pietist influence. Pietistic writings typically used very flowery, emotional language. The blood of Jesus was often spoken about and his death on the cross was a central motif. For example, in an 1808 letter about Johann Wiegand, with whom Waldner had corresponded regularly and who had recently passed away, he wrote that "without doubt a love-bond knotted by the Saviour" existed between him and Wiegand. "Yet I am comforted by one thought: that the loving Saviour adequately sweetened his with comfort and joy." These formulations indicate the influence of Pietism on Johannes Waldner's thinking and theology.

---

30   Ibid, 59.
31   Ibid, 56.

Hutterites and the Moravians found common ground in other areas, such as how to understand repentance, a topic which Johannes Waldner also touched on. A confession of faith he sent to the Moravians contained a chapter entitled, "On the true repentance of the heart," in which the Hutterite elder described the condition of an "anxious and troubled soul." This condition was the prerequisite for a person to recognize the poverty and "nakedness" of his own soul, which had "existed in this world without God until now." Only in this "pitiful predicament," in an "anxious and troubled" state, could the soul perceive the wrath of God, disgrace, and eternal punishment. In order to implement this into the life of faith, one had to come to Jesus Christ with a believing and obedient heart to experience true peace of the soul and "forgiveness" of sins. As a result, the soul would "be born again in essence and in spirit, and would abandon its former sins and turn to God."[32]

Johannes Waldner's ideas and language do not only exhibit similarities with Pietism; one can also observe a connection to Peter Riedemann's *Rechenschaft*, where several passages are also devoted to the theme of repentance. The same applies to *Gelassenheit*, an idea which both Anabaptists and Pietists treasured. The roots of *Gelassenheit* are found in late medieval mysticism, which influenced 16th century Anabaptists. Ulrich Stadler's writing on *Gelassenheit* is perhaps the most well-known Hutterite text on this topic. For Stadler, *Gütergemeinschaft* represented "true *Gelassenheit*;" it was the "highest part and degree" of *Gelassenheit* as well as voluntary submission to God and his people through the Spirit of grace and in the manner of love. In Stadler's words: "willing and ready, makes free and unattached."[33] In the *Codex ritualis*, a Hutterite text used to instruct baptismal candidates, *Gelassenheit* is likewise discussed and defined as detachment from material and worldly possessions.[34] The essential point is summarized in Luke 14:33: "So therefore, none of you can become my disciple if you do not

---

32 Ibid, 64f.
33 Riedemann, *Rechenschaft*, 53,56, 62; Lydia Müller, *Glaubenszeugnisse oberdeutscher Taufgesinnter*, vol. 1, Quellen und Forschungen zur Reformationsgeschichte, vol. 20 (Leipzig: M. Heinsius Nachfolger, 1938), 222.
34 Cod. 213, I-III, Slowakische Akademie der Wissenschaften, fol. 49ʳf.

give up all your possessions."[35] In contrast, the Lutheran theologian Johann Arndt, himself strongly influenced by mysticism and whose publication, *Four Books Concerning true Christianity*, was read in Anabaptist circles, defined *Gelassenheit* as a necessary condition for humans to accept God. He compares the yielded [*gelassene*] soul to still water—it "rests" in God and God in it.

Clearly, Hutterites also embraced other ideas that were central within Pietism, including the concept of a "Philadelphian movement," as it was formulated by the English mystic, Jane Lead. Central for her was the idea that "true believers" who were united by "brotherly love" and were at home in all faith communities and confessions, should be gathered. The letter to the churches in Philadelphia found in Revelations 3 is foundational for this idea: the church in Philadelphia is characterized as possessing a little power and not denying God's word and name and for that reason it receives the promise of protection in the hour of temptation. In this way the awakened ones [*die Erweckten*] in the various churches were united despite confessional boundaries.

In this connection, a passage from a letter written by the Hutterites to Herrnhut in the 1720s is particularly noteworthy; it was exactly the time when the community in Velke Levare was under attack and shortly thereafter had to abandon their *Hof*. Contact with Herrnhut was established after Hutterite Justus Mayer visited the settlement founded by Zinzendorf during his travels. In response, the Hutterites wrote:

> We were very pleased [...] that God does not leave Himself unproven among you, and that you endeavour among yourselves to come close to the orders of the first church. That is also our purpose, but it is not the main thing with us. Rather, we seek to base ourselves and others on Jesus Christ and to experience in our hearts the procreation from above from imperishable seed, from which the sonship of God originates. [...] We believe in an invisible church of Jesus Christ in the Spirit.[36]

---

35 Quoted from: von Schlachta, "*Mit Religions Streitigkeiten*," 67.
36 Müller, *Berührungen*, 212.

This "invisible church of Jesus Christ in the Spirit" is part of the idea pursued by the Philadelphian movement.

Opportunity for Reflection
What role did the old Hutterite traditions play and how did they affect spiritual renewal? Where are traditions upheld today and where do they hinder?

LECTURE THREE
"How can we accept a government authority among us?"[1]

The Hutterites as Political Subjects

Like many other Moravian noblemen, Ulrich von Kaunitz invited Hutterites to settle on his estates. In his last will and testament from 1613 he wrote as follows:

> Do not maliciously expel the Anabaptists and do not revoke from them house nor *Hof*; but, where there are none, don't accept any more. For if it is difficult to live with them, it is even more difficult without them.[2]

This quotation shows the ambivalence which accompanied the toleration of Hutterites. Some 150 years later, the Hutterites appeared on the agenda of two meetings of Empress Maria Theresa's state council in Vienna where it was debated whether the Hutterites should be tolerated in Transylvania or not. Councillor Anton von Stupan advised caution and asked them to consider how Hutterites were important for the economy of Transylvania. His colleague, Egid Felix von Borié, was more wary, associating Hutterites with the Münster rebellion of 1534–35. He argued that unrecognized confessional groups should be quickly suppressed in order to prevent them from growing to the point where they could no longer be contained. The example of Münster had made government officials wary of Anabaptist expansion in their lands.[3]

---

1   Anonymous, "*Verfall der Gemein in Rußland, u. wer schuld ist [The Decline of the Community in Russia, and who is to Blame]*" (n.d., n.p.), 14.
2   Quoted from: Hrúby, *Wiedertäufer in Mähren*, 50.
3   Astrid von Schlachta, *Gefahr oder Segen? Die Täufer in der politischen Kommunika-*

The persecution of Anabaptists was a political issue in the Early Modern period.[4] Though their practice of adult baptism was often mentioned, their alleged political disloyalty was always the primary reason for why Anabaptists should not be tolerated. The reference to Münster, as we have seen, served as a rationale well into the 18th century, an indication of a persistent cultural memory. The mention of the Peasants' War under Thomas Müntzer and the alleged widespread participation of Anabaptists in the fighting contributed to the perception that tolerating Anabaptism was a risky and dangerous matter.

Although Anabaptists were always seen as largely apolitical subjects—they strictly separated the secular and spiritual kingdoms—their overall political history proves to be ambivalent, as the Hutterite example demonstrates. Hutterites had no qualms about getting involved in the world of politics, and in their history Anabaptists appear again and again as active political subjects: whether as holders of government offices, as supporters of a particular party in political conflicts, or as authors of petitions. Thus, already in the early 17th century, Mennonites sat on city councils, and by the 18th century, Mennonites served as *Schulzen*.

Still, these political activities were not uncontroversial inside the community. The title of this lecture—"How can we accept a government authority among us?"—indicates as much: This question originated in a conflict which raged in the 19th century over the influence of *Schulzen*. The *Schulze* represented the government and functioned as a type of mayor in the Molotschna colonies. Hutterites at the time were divided over how much power the *Schulze* should have within the community and to what extent he should participate in the dispensation of justice against community members. Part of the debate included the obligation of the Hutterites, following their migration to the Molotschna, to appoint brothers from within their midst to serve as *Schulzen*.

But first a glimpse into the past: How did Hutterites view political participation in the course of their history? In the context of perse-

---

tion, Schriften zur politischen Kommunikation, vol. 5 (Göttingen: V & R unipress, 2009), 93–100.

4   In general: von Schlachta, *Gefahr oder Segen?*.

cution in the 16th century, Hutterites objected to the influence of political authorities in their community. They strictly divided the spiritual and the political realms, but despite this division and the associated separation, they were obedient to the authorities, as it is laid down in Peter Riedemann's *Rechenschaft*:

> The government is appointed by God as a rod of his anger, to discipline and punish evil and wicked people. [...] One should therefore be obedient to rulers as to those who are appointed by God to protect us, as long as they do not attack the conscience or demand what is against God.[5]

Accordingly, the "Description of the Community" in the *Geschichtbuch* portrays the Hutterite relationship to government in this way:

> They were subject to the authorities and obedient to them in all good works, in all things that were not against God, their faith, or their conscience. They paid their taxes, annual dues, interest, tithes, and custom fees, and they did their compulsory labour. They honoured the governing authorities because of their divinely ordained office, which is as much needed in this wicked world as daily bread.[6]

On the other hand, a closer look at the history shows that in addition to paying the required taxes and services, the community developed good relationships with government representatives—sometimes too cozy. The Hutterites not only had a very good relationship with the lords and nobility during their time in Moravia; there were also situations in which Hutterites were extremely active politically, for example, in 1618 at the beginning of the Thirty Years' War. In the Bohemian territories several noblemen had rebelled against the Habsburg government, resulting in an uprising. The rebels elected their own candidate as King of Bohemia, the Reformed elector, Friedrich von der Pfalz. At the time, the Hutterites clearly supported the rebellious, anti-Habsburg nobility. We

---

5   Riedemann, *Rechenschaft*, 102.
6   *Chronicle*, vol. 1, 404.

know that Hutterite missionaries took along letters sent between the rebels and their supporters in different parts of Germany on their missionary journeys. In addition, Hutterites hosted Friedrich von der Pfalz, newly elected as King by the rebels, on their *Höfen*. They gifted him with goods from their workshops, such as a steel bed, ceramics and knives.

In 1607, Salomon Böger also made use of political channels during the Turkish wars to leverage his success at ransoming Hutterites out of slavery. Another Hutterite, Balthasar Goller, was employed at the time as a doctor in the services of the Habsburg legation in Constantinople. He arranged a position for Salomon Böger in the legation, so he could search for his brothers and sisters in the faith in the Ottoman region. During the 1630s in Transylvania, Hutterites also decreased their distance from the political sphere for a time when they assumed the financial administration for Prince Gábor Bethlen. Further, they allowed themselves to be recruited to participate in a military escort responsible for Bethlen's widow. The alliance which the Hutterites in the 16th century made with the nobility remained a blueprint for Hutterite existence in the Early Modern period.[7]

Moreover, during an interrogation conducted by the Jesuit cathedral preacher Lamprecht, the Hutterite missionary [*Sendbote*] Hans Arbeiter, who was imprisoned in Speyer in 1568, praised the good relationship Hutterites had with the nobility and the emperor. He demonstrated that these people learned to value "our conduct and life very much" and "also often brought aristocratic men and women to tour and see our houses and schools and other facilities." Other sources also indicate regular visits by members of the nobility. According to Arbeiter, a government that tolerated Hutterites would be granted

> everything commanded by God, and what God prescribed as appropriate for such an office, such as taxes, interest, custom fees, duties on our goods, and compulsory labour [*fronnen oder roboeten*]. We gladly and willingly give to the government, and

---

7   von Schlachta, *Hutterische Konfession*, 296; von Schlachta, *From the Tyrol to North America*, 79.

strive to give anybody what we owe them before God. We also help to build and repair roads and streets and treat everybody in a way that does not conflict with God and love of neighbour.[8]

A debate in 1599 illustrates the kinds of specific questions and problems this close relationship with the nobility presented. In this year, Franz von Dietrichstein, the lord of Nikolsburg, where Hutterites lived, was appointed bishop of Olmütz. This was a moral dilemma for the Hutterites, who considered whether they could continue working for Franz von Dietrichstein. The elders questioned whether the services the community offered Dietrichstein would too closely associate them with 'Catholic clergy,' which could, in turn, become a gateway for Catholic ideas to flow into the community. Following several debates, the leaders came to the conclusion that Franz von Dietrichstein "either had to be recognized as a lord and authority, or to relocate the communities on his estates." The latter obviously proved to be the less attractive option and was rejected on the grounds of not creating unrest in the land, "which might not contribute to God's praise and the wellbeing of the faithful." The leaders reached a compromise which approved working for Franz von Dietrichstein on his Nikolsburg estates, but not on his episcopal estates. Work associated with the bishop's castle in Kremsier was to be avoided. According to the *Geschicht-Buch*, Dietrichstein reacted angrily when he learned about the Hutterite decision.[9]

However, the compromise did not last long. A short time later, the Hutterites agreed to build a mill for Dietrichstein. Even though the mill was on his Nikolsburg estate and financed by money he insisted was not connected to the bishop's office, the Hutterite craftsmen continued working at the Kremsier bishopric once the construction of the mill was complete. They built ovens, clocks, and worked on other jobs—apparently, without informing the elders. In 1604, this issue appeared on the agenda of the great assembly, which took place at Neumühl and was attended by all ministers,

---

8   Quoted from: von Schlachta, *Hutterische Konfession*, 293f.
9   *Chronicle*, vol. 1, 549–552.

Haushalter, as well as other brothers and craftsmen. The community's *Ältester*, Klaus Braidl, sharply criticized the fact that

> several brothers had associated too closely and grown too comfortable with heretical groups [*falsche Völker*], especially with the Catholic clergy and had used, obeyed and observed the policy of separation too little.[10]

An incident from a later time suggests that this debate was likely not unique. As already mentioned in the previous lecture, during the 1770s Matthias Hofer not only generated debates about the manner of prayer within the Hutterite community, but also concerning relations with governing authorities. Hofer tried to convince his brothers and sisters not to tip their hat when greeting secular authorities, and "that one should also not greet any non-believers." Additionally, he insisted that believers should not be employed by a "non-believer," because that would support their selfish interests. Hofer's statements challenged the leaders to search the *Geschichts-Buch* for how Hutterites had dealt with these questions in the past. With respect to the question about greeting authorities they came to the conclusion that in the past the community had no problems with it and it was decided "in these points to stay with the old understanding and *Ordnung*."[11]

The practical arrangement of their relationship with the governing authorities was an ongoing issue for Hutterites. In the Molotschna, where the Hutterites settled in 1842, the debate broke out with greater intensity, because in South Russia they had to assume political offices, which wreaked havoc with the community's structures. But first a look back at the circumstances surrounding the migration to the Molotschna.

The Joining of the Carinthian Transmigrants and the Consequences

With the joining of the Carinthian Crypto-Protestants, also known as transmigrants, the Hutterite community—which had given up *Gütergemeinschaft* at the beginning of the 18th century and whose

---
10   *Chronicle*, vol. 1, 567–572.
11   *Chronicle*, vol. 2, 468f, 487.

numbers had shrunk considerably—experienced a revival of their confessional heritage. The sources indicate that the *Ältester* Joseph Kuhr regularly read to the newcomers from the old Hutterite texts and gave them a variety of Hutterite books to read, so they could form their own opinion. Among these books were Peter Riedemann's *Rechenschaft*, the *Handbüchlein wider den Prozeß, der zu Worms am Rheine wider die Brüder, so man die Hutterischen nennt, ausgangen ist im 1557. Jahr [Handbook Opposing the Trial Conducted at Worms on the Rhine Against the Brothers which are called Hutterites, published in 1557]*, as well as a collection of various texts from the 16th century, which came to be known as *"Übrige Brocken [Leftover Crumbs]."* **Übrige Brocken** consisted of a letter from Hans Kräl to Melchior Platzer, several prayers and a letter the Hutterites wrote to the Swiss Brethren in 1567, which originated as part of a very controversial and polemical debate.

The Swiss Brethren were an Anabaptist group that established congregations in Switzerland and in southwestern Germany and had called themselves 'Mennonites' since the late 17th century. During the 16th century they engaged in several debates with the Hutterites about matters of faith, on which the two communities had different views. Among these issues were *Gütergemeinschaft*, the treatment of those who wanted to leave Hutterite communities, offices in the community, divorce, the education of children, as well as the payment of taxes, and shunning. In 1565 the Hutterites answered a very long letter from the Swiss Brethren with a letter totalling 189 folios. Both texts contain a significant level of polemic directed against the other group. The Hutterites had hoped the Swiss Brethren would join them, but this did not happen. Now, the letter served the purpose of providing the Carinthian Crypto-Protestants with the "basics" about the community's faith foundations and organization.[12] Interestingly, at this time the *"Allgemeine Dienstordnung* [General Offices' *Ordnung*]" of 1580 was adopted to once again organize the life of the community according to the old Hutterite structures. At the beginning of the 1760s, the Hutterites also reintroduced *Gütergemeinschaft*.

---

12   John D. Roth, "The Hutterites and Swiss Brethren in Debate (1567): The Persistence of Competing Traditions" (unpublished paper, 1994); von Schlachta, *Hutterische Konfession*, 191–195.

But the Hutterites now faced a problem. They came under the scrutiny of the Habsburg authorities because uniting with the Carinthian Protestants was considered to be an act of proselytizing. This once again brought persecution or the repressive measures of recatholication into their lives. In 1763, Maria Theresa, who also ruled the Holy Roman Empire of the German Nation with her husband, Emperor Francis I, released an order that the Hutterites should no longer be tolerated in Transylvania. Their ministers were to lose their right to preach and the community was to leave the country within six weeks or convert to Catholicism. At the same time, Maria Theresa introduced a Jesuit mission whose agents single-mindedly worked against the Hutterites. The Jesuits forced the Hutterites to attend services conducted by priest Johann Theophil Delpini in the Hutterite *Bethaus*. It is said that *Ältester* Joseph Kuhr resisted these measures on several occasions and refused to attend the compulsory church services. For these actions he was imprisoned.

Other Hutterites offered less resistance, yielding to the pressure and converting to the Catholic faith, as was the case during the expulsion from Moravia. Like in Moravia, the recatholization attempts in Transylvania began with the children. For this purpose, an orphanage was established in Hermannstadt, not only for orphans, but for children who had a parent who was "non-Catholic." Since this policy also affected Hutterite families, the Hutterites increasingly thought about migrating once again, but the planning had to be done secretly.

Yet the trials and tribulations confronting the Hutterites did not only come from the outside; in this final phase in Transylvania the community faced problems which plagued them again and again throughout their history. If the decline of *Gütergemeinschaft* is a constant theme in Hutterite history, then slander from former members now also becomes a recurring problem. This was already the case in Moravia and continued in the 17th century. Dissatisfied members left the community and spread nasty rumours and reports in order to inflict the greatest possible damage on Hutterites. This was the case with Georg Geissy, the leader who took a large share of the community's property when he left, leveling a serious economic blow against the community.

Now, in the 1750s there were also instances where Hutterites left the community and subsequently harshly criticized and slandered it, tarnishing their public image. Johann Foltin from the community at Alwinz is one such example. He expressed criticism against the *Ältesten*, but unfortunately, we do not know exactly what he criticized. The Hutterites, however, viewed their reputation so damaged, that they sued him for libel and evil slander. The court sided with the Hutterites and sentenced Foltin to pay a fine. In this context it is also interesting that the Hutterites took legal action at all, since the community had always shied away from resolving conflicts through the courts.[13]

Thus, the situation had worsened considerably for the Hutterites. The adults were threatened with imprisonment if they refused to convert to Catholicism, and the children would be brought into an orphanage, where they would be raised according to "right teaching." Therefore, a group of Hutterites decided to leave Transylvania in 1767 and to flee to Walachei, and from there, to Wischenky.

New Organization and Growing Traditionalism in Wallachia

The pattern of the expulsion from Moravia repeated itself in many ways in Transylvania. It was again a nobleman, Count Peter Rumjanzew-Sadunaisky, who accepted the Hutterites and gave them land in Wischenky because it promised to be economically beneficial for him. In this situation the Hutterites also benefited from Early Modern law, which allowed political tolerance to be granted apart from the empire's laws and regulations, if a lord or nobleman granted it. In Wischenky, the Hutterites received privileges which aimed to make settlement attractive. Thus, they were granted exemption from military service and from swearing oaths. Count Rumjanzew-Sadunaisky also allowed them to live and work together as communities, and granted them a three-year exemption from taxes such as the tithe so they could build up their community and

---

13   von Schlachta, *From the Tyrol to North America*, 97–100.

industries. Moreover, they received wood for construction and financial support to cover migration costs among others.

Internal reorganization also took place in Wischenky, as a series of *Gemeindeordnungen* reveals. It appears that Hutterite life was very quickly defined by a thoroughgoing traditionalism. According to a report from the Moravian Brethren at Sarepta, written by Johann Wiegand several years later, the Hutterites could be recognized by the conformity of their clothing. Additionally, they permit few changes in their life, always say the same prayers, and observe the same daily routine. Wiegand reports further that in the community there was an "exaggerated aversion to everything new and contemporary." He asserts that every innovation was viewed suspiciously, which was very damaging for the community.[14]

This traditionalism and conformity in dress is also apparent in the *Gemeindeordnungen*. In an *Ordnung* from 1775, the elders of the community exhorted the members:

> The brothers at Vishenka met to talk about the way the sisters made garments, because a number of sisters do not make the same kind of apron as the others, but introduce new fashions. The elder brothers decided that the old style should be kept and no new ones introduced; the sisters should not make slashed jackets with different colored insets but be content with what is given them. If any sister should fail to observe the kindly warning and advice, discipline would have to follow.[15]

With respect to clothing, everything should remain as the old *Ordnung* prescribed; innovations were to be non-existent. The descriptions of the offices in the community also shows adherence to the traditions of the 16th and 17th centuries as the *Allgemeine Dienstordnung* of 1580 continued to orient the community. Yet in Wischenky an *Ordnung* with the following content was created:

> Brothers who go to market—whether they are arti-

---

14   *Chronicle*, vol. 2, 599.
15   Ibid, 798f.

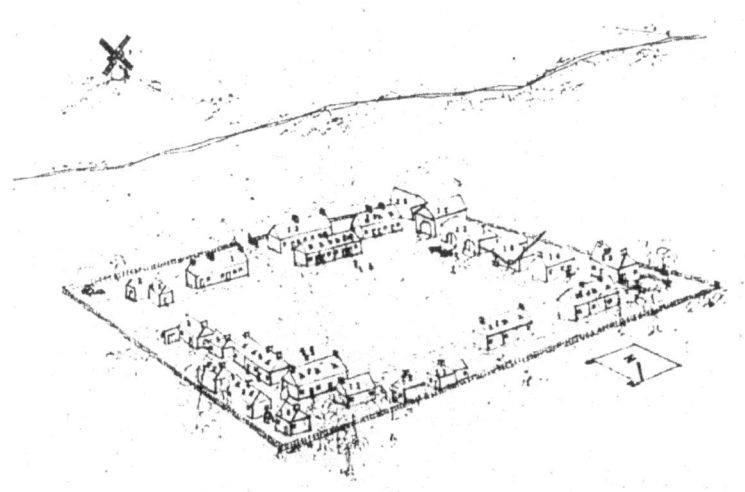

A drawing by W.P. Thompson of Radiceva according to a written description from 1818.
[SOURCE: Paul Thompson, Hutterite Community: Artefact Art, Vol I, Part II, Thesis, Cornell University, 1977.]

sans or others who are sent by the steward to make purchases—should not take the liberty to buy their wives and children quantities of good things to eat. If they occasionally want to buy something, it is their duty to give an account of every penny to the steward. But they are not to so overdo their purchasing that it causes unhappiness and annoyance to those who never have the opportunity to get out.[16]

For Hutterites the challenge remained: to live responsibly and maturely in community.

Until 1802, the Hutterites lived in Wischenky. Following Count Rumjanzew-Sadunaisky's death, the Hutterites were involved in a conflict with his sons, which resulted in Hutterites having to migrate once again. The destination this time was Radiceva, which was not very far from Wischenky. Like in Wischenky, in Radiceva the Hutterites fell under Russian rule as the highest level of government; previously they had always lived under Austrian, or Habsburg rule. Here in Radiceva, Hutterites lived directly on crown

---

16   Ibid, 805f.

land for the first time, and in this respect they were more tightly bound up with the political administration, since they now had to appoint their own *Schulzen*. It appears that assuming such a political office in Radiceva did not initially cause problems.

Nevertheless, in Wallachia the community was also not spared from internal disagreements and divisions; since the first decade of the 19th century, times became more difficult for Hutterites. Towards the end of his life, Johannes Waldner, who not only played a pivotal role in the reorganization of the community, but also ensured that the writing of the *Chronicle* was continued, came into conflict with Jacob Walter. Walter had fled to Wallachia from Upper Hungary after the Hutterites there were forcibly recatholized and not permitted to return to their old Hutterite faith in the 1780s. Walter rose in prominence to become a leader and assistant to Johannes Waldner. He also accompanied Waldner to St. Petersburg in 1801 in order to negotiate privileges for the Hutterites and to seek a new location for the community.

With Jacob Walter, a new generation of leaders who had a different concept of communal life than Johannes Waldner came to power. Even though the specific practice of *Gütergemeinschaft* was at the centre of the conflict, the issue of power between the generations might have been particularly influential: the younger Jacob Walter against the older Johannes Waldner. The *Klein-Geschichtbuch* reports about this development in hindsight:

> The last and greatest misfortune leading to the community's downfall—diligently promoted by Satan—was that Johannes Waldner, servant of the Word and the Elder of the church, became disunited with Jacob Walter, the assistant servant of the Word. The community was split into two almost equal camps by this division between the Elder, who clung with all his might to the system of community-of-goods, and his younger assistant, who rejected this old and honoured Hutterian tradition. Both ministers held to their own view with equal obstinacy.[17]

---

17   *Chronicle*, vol. 2, 614.

Among other things, *Ältester* Johannes Waldner accused Walter of showing special favour towards his own family and thus undermining the idea of *Gütergemeinschaft*. Moreover, there were several deficiencies in the community's life which Walter and his supporters considered irremediable, which led them to question the whole idea of *Gütergemeinschaft*.

Consequently, Jacob Walter and his brother Darius separated themselves from the community at Radiceva, moved into a nearby house, and demanded their share of the community's property. These conflicts led to a new decline of the Hutterite community. At the end of the second decade of the 19th century Hutterites once again gave up *Gütergemeinschaft*. This development, together with division in the congregation, brought much distress and poverty to the community. There are accounts from 1818 that the community's homes were very run-down.[18] The communal dining hall, kitchen, and school were described as unclean. The air was stuffy and heavy which resulted in many of the children becoming sick.

Thus, the person of Johannes Waldner—who was *Ältester* for 31 years and a Servant of the Word for 42 years—represents, on one hand, consolidation of the Hutterite community following the arrival of the Carinthian transmigrants and an openness towards other confessions. On the other hand, he represents a transition into a new time—the 19th century—which raised new questions for Hutterites. How can Johannes Waldner be characterized? It is certainly not incorrect to characterize him as spiritually open, which can be seen by his contacts with the Moravian Brethren. In addition, the observations which he regularly inserted in his writing of the *Klein-Geschichtbuch* show that he was open to try out new spiritual forms, and thankful when every single Hutterite personally read the Bible:

> The gatherings for prayer and especially the reading at midday helped build up the young people's faith. As previously described, each read in turn and so each was involved, and it often led to a talk about

---

18 Aleksandr Augustovič Klaus, *Unsere Kolonien: Studien und Materialien zur Geschichte und Statistik der ausländischen Kolonisation in Russland* (Odessa, 1887), 71.

the meaning of a passage of Holy Scripture. At that time each one took pains to be able to read out the Scripture fluently, and such a practice should still be used with a good conscience today.[19]

Johannes Waldner's Moravian Brethren correspondence partner, Johann Wiegand, characterized him as "far more liberal than his congregation" and observed that this would continue to cause friction within his community.[20] However, in his vision for the Hutterites, Johannes Waldner seems to have adopted a rather conservative position. He felt closely attached to the traditions of the 16th and 17th century Hutterites, and often took his cues and examples from history. In conflicts and debates over the right way to live as a community of faith his attention went back to the past and the written legacy of the Hutterites. Despite his efforts, at the end of Waldner's time as elder, the community fell into a severe crisis.

In order to deal with the ongoing decline of the community in Radiceva, the Hutterites once again looked for an alternative place to live. This time an escape route opened up in the Molotschna, a region in Southern Russia near the Black Sea, where the Mennonites had settled. The Mennonites were a great help to the Hutterites, especially the Mennonite leader Johann Cornies, who advocated for the Hutterites with the authorities and vouched for the financially unstable settlers. The Mennonites supported the Hutterites with the construction of their homes, with the preparation of the fields, and with all other matters relating to political and social integration.[21]

The Hutterites Between Integration and Separation—Questions Regarding Political Participation

The move to the Molotschna and the settlement in the Mennonite colonies brought several changes for the Hutterites. They had to adjust to new social structures and integrate themselves into the system of self-administration which had developed among the

---

19 *Chronicle*, vol. 2, 504f.
20 Ibid, 599. "Authentische Nachricht von den so genannten Hutterischen Brüdern in der Ukraine," *Christliche Zeitschrift für Christen* 3 (1811): 139.
21 David H. Epp, *Johann Cornies* (Rosthern/Steinbach: Echo Verlag, 1946).

Mennonites in the region. This political integration meant that settlers had to develop policies themselves and participate in political administration. Like the Mennonites, Hutterites were required to nominate a *Schulze* and two assessors [*Beisitzer*] to look after political matters. Having to assume responsibility for these three positions reawakened the question surrounding political participation among the Hutterites and created intense internal debates. A 'Yes' response would have meant that the Christian-Hutterite faith was not sharply distinct from the political realm which had been the community's practice up to that point and required by Peter Riedemann's *Rechenschaft*, among others. A 'no' response would have made settlement in the Molotschna impossible.

Because of this, a discussion began within the Hutterite community about how to deal with these political requirements and two problems arose. First, the fact that a Hutterite exercised the position of *Schulze*. This had already been the case in Radiceva, but had not resulted in any conflicts—only in the Molotschna did debates erupt. This probably had to do with the second problem, namely the fact that other *Schulzen* from villages where Hutterites lived, began to exert their authority more strongly in the community. The fact that the Hutterites now had political administrators in their own ranks, or were more closely linked to the political authorities, also meant they had to cede part of the jurisdiction that had belonged to the community to secular authorities. Earlier, leaders had resolved conflicts within the community and enforced community discipline.

Further, as Christians, Hutterites also had rules not to appear before secular courts, though, their position changed from time to time, as several court cases in Transylvania indicate. In contrast, an account from the late 18th century reports that the Hutterites would not bring "quarrels and legal matters" before the government. This is described by the Mennonite Heinrich Donner from west Prussian Ohrlofferfelde, who wrote his report after conversations with Hutterites, Joseph Müller and Christian Hofer. When Müller and Hofer visited the west Prussian Mennonites in 1783, Donner was amazed that Joseph Müller did not know the first thing about the word "trial." He describes how he clarified the word for Müller and how he questioned him whether any conflicts ever develop among the Hutterites, to which Müller responded:

> No, because "mine-and-thine" has ended among us, no such conflicts happen, and when something does come up, we resolve it on our own, according to the command in 1 Corinthians 6:1–6. Thus, we have nothing to do with the government, other than paying the obligatory taxes. Should anybody seek protection or legal rights from the government, he would no longer be considered a member.[22]

Historically, Hutterites had settled disputes which actually belonged to the secular jurisdiction within their community through their own judicial process. Now, in the Molotschna, this was no longer possible. The *Schulze*, whom Hutterites had to appoint, took over these tasks and the community lost a degree of agency. The *Schulze* now also had power over the *Ältester*, which was new for the Hutterites; he could even punish the *Ältester*. In addition, the Hutterites had to use forms of punishment that were not common within the community, such as caning [*Stockschläge*]. All these changes resulted in arguments and factions among the Hutterites. Some Hutterites sided with the political authorities and the Mennonites, cultivated regular fellowship with them, and voiced their desire for greater political participation. Others rejected extensive contact and pleaded for a stricter separation. Among others, David Jantzen, a Mennonite school master in a Hutterite school, faced accusations that he negatively influenced the community. Another recurring issue was the fact that Hutterites were labelled as "Mennonites" in official documents and treated as such; they did not want to be lumped together.

The person of Johann Cornies is responsible for the growing, and in some respects very extensive, influence of the Mennonites on the Hutterites. He was an influential man in the Molotschna, had no qualms about engaging with mainstream society, and established good contacts with many political officials. Cornies was the highest authority in community affairs and at the same time an innovative

---

22   Donner, *Kurzer Bericht*, 85.

and progressive Mennonite. He provoked reforms in agriculture and education, which also had influence on the direction of the Hutterite community. On the one hand, Hutterites conformed to the ideas of Cornies and learned much about agriculture in the Molotschna. On the other hand, countless conflicts raged around the person of Cornies, suggesting a struggle involving power and competence. To be fair, it needs to be mentioned that Cornies also generated a lot of conflict in his own Mennonite circles.

The question of political participation was put in concrete terms for the Hutterites when dealing with the position of *Schulze*. A vigorous debate erupted after Hutterite Johannes Wipf was accused of getting into a fight with a Russian servant.[23] The court declared him guilty and sentenced him to be disciplined by the Mennonite *Schulze* of Blumenort, who was to punish Wipf with a beating. The Hutterites protested this punishment and, in the process, it also came to light that the community was divided on the question of whether to recognize the authorities. The conflict ignited when Johann Cornies demanded that all affected individuals sign a petition declaring their recognition of the political authorities. Once again this resulted in intense debates among the Hutterites.

Samuel Kleinsasser was strongly opposed to signing such a document, arguing:

> How can we recognize an authority among us? Christ teaches his disciples in Luke 22:25–26, "The kings of the Gentiles lord it over them; and those in authority over them are called benefactors. But not so with you."

Romans 12:19 furnished a further argument: "Beloved, never avenge yourselves, but leave room for the wrath of God; for it is written, 'Vengeance is mine, I will repay, says the Lord.'" The opposing party, which included David and Jakob Hofer, likewise referred to Bible verses, quoting Romans 13:1: "Let every person be subject to the governing authorities; for there is no authority except from God, and those authorities that exist have been insti-

---

23 The following events as reported in: Anonymous, *Verfall der Gemein*.

tuted by God." The lines of conflict were drawn. The waves swelled and accusations increased. Thus, Kleinsasser accused the Hofers of "depending on people from the world [*Welt Menschen*], namely on Cornies."[24]

A further debate emerged about whether one could even call somebody who assumed the position of *Schulze* a "brother." The school master David Jantzen suggested a Solomon-like solution: "When there is a meeting involving the *Schulze*, he is not your brother. Then he is part of the government, and when the meeting is over, the *Schulze* is your brother once again." The conflict festered for some time and the aged *Ältester* Jacob Walter also became involved. He was imprisoned, apparently because of his refusal to recognize the government. Especially controversial was the fact that several Hutterites were present when he was arrested and they did not interfere because they disagreed with Walter. Thus, the question about how much power the secular government should have within the Hutterite community generated plenty of friction. Jacob Walter defended the opposing position with a strict division of the two kingdoms while another part of the community no longer took the separation between worldly and spiritual kingdoms as seriously.[25]

There were further conflicts with Johann Cornies, who acted as the representative of the political authorities, regarding certain Hutterite practices. For example, the group that wanted to reintroduce *Gütergemeinschaft* in the 1840s landed in conflict with the Mennonites. This intention was met with resistance from the secular authorities and Johann Cornies.[26] Only after the death of Cornies in 1848 did the communally-minded Hutterites pursue it again. Thus, some Hutterites lived in private property, namely in Hutterthal, Johannesruh, and Neu-Hutterthal, while in Hutterdorf and Scheromet some Hutterites had settled into *Gütergemeinschaft*. Michel Waldner, the "founder" of the Schmiedeleut, for example, lived in Scheromet. While ill, he had had a vision that the community ought to live according to the old *Ordnungen*. The mes-

---

24 von Schlachta, *From the Tyrol to North America*, 150–152.
25 *Verfall der Gemein*, 47.
26 Astrid von Schlachta, "A new-old-identity? Influences and interaction between Mennonites and Hutterites in South Russia," *Molochna 2004. Mennonites and their Neighbours, 1804–2004*, (Zaporizhia, 2004), 168–172.

Fifty years after immigrating to America, David Hofer returned to his birth place in Johannesruh. [SOURCE: David Hofer, *Die Hungersnot in Russland und unsere Reise um die Welt* (Chicago, 1924).]

senger in the vision said, "The ark is the community of the Holy Spirit, which you do not practice any longer." Waldner took this admonition to heart and revived communal living.[27]

Another century-old Hutterite custom, their marriage practice, was debated and abolished in the 19th century under pressure from the Mennonites and Johann Cornies. Since the 16th century, it was common among Hutterites to conduct marriages through arrangement by the leaders. A fascinating glimpse into this Hutterite practice is offered by a report associated with an inheritance claim processed before the Imperial Court Council in Vienna.[28] The matter involved a citizen of the city of Kaufbeuren who raised a claim to his father's inheritance. His father had traveled to Moravia, joined the Hutterites and passed away while there. In order to investigate the legal situation, the city of Kaufbeuren sent a messenger to Moravia to learn about the life and faith of the Hutterites. During his visit to Nikolschitz he discovered that the Hutterite leaders arranged the marriages. When a man had the intention to get married, he informed the leaders and they looked for a wife for

---

27 *Anfang von den Hutterischen Schmieden Gemeinden* (Hawley: Spring Prairie Printing, 1986), 5.
28 von Schlachta, *Gefahr oder Segen?*, 156–158.

him. The leaders asked those who wanted to get married whether they "desired and willed" to get married. According to the report, "nobody was forced or required to accept the other." Following spiritual instruction from the *Ältesten*, the couple was married by means of a handshake before a gathering of the community. This practice from the 16th century was still in effect in the 19th century. In the Molotschna, Hutterite members themselves criticized this way of conducting marriages. Several young Hutterites resisted and appealed to Johann Cornies for help and after his intervention, the Hutterites gave up their old marriage practice.[29]

Contacts with the Mennonites

Thus, the influence of Mennonites on Hutterites in the Molotschna was extensive. Yet these experiences in South Russia were not the first intensive contacts between Hutterites and Mennonites. In times of crisis the Hutterites had often turned to the Mennonites; next to the Moravian Brethren, they were the second most important contact group. This was already the case in the 17th century, as a 1665 letter to the Dutch Mennonites indicates. The letter originated at a time when the pressure on the community in Transylvania was increasing due to the Turkish Wars, and besides this, a fire in Sabatisch had destroyed many workshops.[30]

The letter's primary aim was to request financial support from the Dutch Mennonites. To place more weight on the request, two Hutterites travelled to the Netherlands to personally deliver it and give a report about their situation. By the middle of the 17th century, the addressees of the letter, the Dutch Mennonites, were already well-integrated in urban society. In addition, they had amassed considerable wealth through their commerce and shipping businesses, so that the Hutterites had reason to be hopeful about receiving money and support from them. And apparently the Hutterite strategy was successful, as a letter from several decades later shows. In the 1740s, when the Hutterites once again turned to the Men-

---

29 von Schlachta, *A new-old-identity?*.
30 *Chronicle*, vol. 1, 792–798.

nonites for help, they referenced the letter of 1665 and the "generous contribution" which the community had received at the time.[31]

Besides the fact that the Hutterites turned to the Mennonites during a time of need, there is another very interesting detail in the 1665 letter. The Hutterites address the Mennonites as "very worthy friends, brothers and sisters in the Lord."[32] This formulation would never have been used in the 16th century, because based on an exclusive understanding of their respective communities, the early Anabaptists did not consider each other as brothers and sisters. This is also underscored by the goal of Hutterite mission to win other Anabaptists, such as the Swiss Brethren, for communal life in Moravia. Yet there are two other possible reasons why the Hutterites chose this way of addressing the Mennonites. On the one hand, they might have been motivated by the fact that they wanted money, so they ignored confessional differences in order to give their request more weight. On the other hand, addressing the Mennonites as "brothers and sisters" could be an indication that Hutterites at the time were really open for deeper contacts beyond their own confessional boundaries and were actually seeking fraternal connections with members from related faith traditions.

In any case, this was the determining motive in their contacts with the Moravian Brethren in the 18th century. As Hutterites at the end of the 1740s sought to renew the connection with the Mennonites in the Netherlands, they also emphasized their yearning for mutual edification and encouragement. Upon getting a response from the Mennonites, Hutterite *Ältester* Zacharias Walter expressed his joy in a letter, writing it was "as if we had heard from God's angels."[33] The Mennonites sent several theological and devotional texts to the Hutterites, among them excerpts from the most notable writings of Menno Simons compiled by Johannes Deknatel, a Mennonite

---

31 Quoted from: Astrid von Schlachta, "Als ob man uns von engeln gottes saget:" Ein Netzwerk konfessionell devianter Untertanen im 18. Jahrhundert," *Konfessionen und Kulturen in der Frühen Neuzeit*, Kaspar v. Greyerz and Thomas Kaufmann, eds. (Heidelberg: Verein für Reformationsgeschichte, 2008), 217.
32 *Chronicle*, vol. 1, 792.
33 Quoted from: von Schlachta, "Als ob man uns von engeln gottes saget," 201.

from the Netherlands.³⁴ Eighteenth-century Hutterites also read books which Quaker missionaries brought to Upper Hungary.

The correspondence in the 1740s did not put an end to Mennonite-Hutterite connections, instead they became even more intensive and personal, as several Hutterites joined the Mennonites in West Prussia in the 1780s.³⁵ In Upper Hungary the political pressure against Hutterites had increased; community members had fled to Wallachia as well as to the Mennonites in West Prussia. In order to visit these Hutterites, Joseph Müller and Christian Hofer decided to make a detour to West Prussia on a trip in 1783. They intended to both visit their co-religionists and discuss faith and life with the Mennonites. They visited many Mennonite communities, participated in intensive discussions, and preached in Mennonite worship services. Apparently, they very successfully advertised their communal life, because several Mennonites joined them on the journey back to South Russia. In his report on the visit, Heinrich Donner wrote that Hofer preached on Ephesians 10:4–12 in a Mennonite church. His assessment was that "the language was somewhat foreign high German, but the homily was biblical and edifying."³⁶

A year later news came from the Mennonite community of Ellerwald that more refugees from Upper Hungary had arrived, after which Johannes Waldner and Jacob Walter made their way north as well. Once again there were intense discussions with the Mennonites—among other topics—about *Gemeinschaft*, where the very different understandings of both communities were once again debated. Hutterites understood *Gemeinschaft* as a requirement for all Christians while Mennonites were of the opinion that "living in common" was also practiced when those in need were supported.³⁷

Judging by the letters that were sent back and forth following the discussions, Hutterites and Mennonites clashed mightily with each other, testing the proclaimed "brotherly and sisterly spirit [*Geschwisterschaft*]." A letter written by Johannes Waldner, Joseph Müller

34   Johannes Deknatel, ed., *Auszug der merkwürdigsten Abhandlungen aus den Werken Menno Simons*, (Büdingen, 1758).
35   Regarding the various contacts, see: von Schlachta, *Täufer*, 219–222.
36   Donner, *Kurzer Bericht*, 44.
37   *Gemeindeblatt der Mennoniten* (1876), 44.

and Joseph Kuhr to the Mennonite Gerhard Wiebe in 1785, addressed the rift that had developed. The Hutterites turned to nasty rhetorical barbs, accusing the Mennonites of "arrogance, individualism, and excess." Their attitude toward trade and commerce—buying and selling—was not consistent with their Christian witness. The Hutterites viewed trade and commerce as unchristian, while the Mennonites had no misgivings about it. They had become prosperous through commerce in big cities such as Amsterdam or Danzig. For the Hutterites, Mennonite life was completely unjust —and justice can have no fellowship with injustice. The Hutterites concluded that the Mennonites were "not perfect" in abiding by the "teachings of Christ." Thus, they ran the risk of not being able to stand before God in the end. Interestingly, all these condemnations did not hinder the Hutterites from emphasizing that there should be "no animosity among us or between us;" rather they desired to "continue on with you by encouraging love and good works." They expressed the hope that Mennonites would decide "to pursue completeness" and abandon their "unchristian" position.[38]

How the Mennonites in turn viewed the Hutterites can be seen in remarks made by Mennonite Gerhard Wiebe in a letter he wrote to his brother Lorenz Friedenreich in Neuwied in 1786. He wrote that Joseph Müller had preached in "an edifying way" during his first visit, but Johannes Waldner and Jacob Walter, who came to West Prussia in 1784, were "somewhat more bearable" than Müller and Hofer—apparently a reflection of the particularly intense discussions. He reports further that they had good conversations, but were particularly divided about *Gütergemeinschaft*. Wiebe writes that when it is practiced out of love, *Gütergemeinschaft* was in order, but not when love was absent—an accusation he likely made against the Hutterites. He also noted that the Hutterites did not tolerate commerce; they were only craftsmen and agrarians. The Mennonite concludes that they departed "not fully as brothers," but as "dear friends."[39]

---

38 Johannes Waldner, Joseph Müller and Joseph Kuhr to Gerhard Wiebe, 1785. A copy is held at the Mennonitische Forschungsstelle Weierhof, C.26, Christian Neff collection, box 19, folder 138.
39 *Letters from Lorentz Friedenreich*, Vol. 4, 45.

These contacts had interesting repercussions. As already mentioned, it appears the Hutterite visitors in West Prussia had so convincingly depicted communal life that several Mennonites joined the community in Wischenky. However, not with lasting success, for according to Hutterite sources, many of the Mennonites committed too early and too eagerly to the Hutterite experiment, without calculating the costs associated with such a life. These Mennonites had enthusiastically sold everything and moved joyfully to the Hutterites, only to wake up to reality in Wischenky after a while. "It didn't last long before reports were heard that they didn't like it. The work was too strenuous, the food too meagre, and besides they had this and that to expose."[40] The Hutterites had tried to prepare newcomers by introducing a period of probation before fully joining the community, as the *Klein-Geschichtbuch* documents. They presented the Mennonites with the same ten points that Hutterite baptismal candidates received and

> specially advised them to send two or more members from their congregation to gain an idea of the structure and daily order of the community and the manner of life of the brothers and sisters; if these representatives became convinced that the life was given by God, they could then take the next steps on the way their hearts told them to follow. They promised to do this.[41]

In addition those interested in joining were asked to read Peter Riedemann's *Rechenschaft*. Though the exchange between the Hutterites and Mennonites in the 18th century was intense and polemical—but also disappointing—the relationship becomes even more important in the first half of the 19th century.

The Hutterites in Upper Hungary—"Hutterites" and "Habaner"

How did Hutterites in Upper Hungary—the second region where Hutterites lived in the 18th century—fare at this time? It has already been mentioned several times that some Hutterites from

---

40   *Chronicle*, vol. 2, 565f.
41   Ibid, 564.

there fled to the Wallachia, for example Jacob Walter, who became the assistant to, and later the adversary of Johannes Waldner. The history of Hutterites in Upper Hungary must be painted in very bleak colours; it was not without several tragic developments. The Hutterites in Upper Hungary in the second half of the 18th century were as threatened as their brothers and sisters in Transylvania. The community in Upper Hungary also had to endure strong external pressure, exerted through mandates which revoked tolerance of Hutterites, and by a Jesuit mission. More and more Hutterites converted to Catholicism, often through force, but sometimes also willingly, as became apparent in conflicts that arose during the 1780s. These conflicts between various factions of ex-Hutterites brought forth nasty human behaviours: defamation and denunciation characterized the relations between former brothers and sisters.

The problems in Upper Hungary had already begun in the 1720s. The fact that Hutterites made contact with the Moravian Brethren at that time had to do with these problems, among other things. In the 1720s, Hutterites had to give up the *Hof* in Velke Levare for a short time due to a change in ownership; a Jesuit mission created additional difficulties and the community was also accused of wanting to storm Velke Levare's castle—presumably an accusation that again emphasized the alleged political disloyalty of the Hutterites. The Hutterites were able to come to an agreement with their landlord and return to their farm, but they had to make confessional concessions. They were no longer allowed to use their prayer house and had to introduce child baptism—the first time in Hutterite history that baptism of faith was abandoned. An 80-verse song published in *Die Lieder der Hutterischen Brüder* tells of this time.[42] However, the sources suggest that the Hutterites actually became "Anabaptists" again in the decades that followed. Although they baptized their children as Catholics, they encouraged them to be secretly baptized into the Hutterite faith at a reasonable age.

---

42   Josef Beck, *Die Geschichts-Bücher der Wiedertäufer in Oesterreich-Ungarn* (Wien, 1883), 566–569; von Schlachta, Gefahr oder Segen?, 386–393; *Die Lieder der Hutterischen Brüder* (Scottdale, 1914), 879–885.

In the 1760s, however, the pressure in Upper Hungary worsened—exactly at the time when the Hutterites in Transylvania were also in need. Once again it was a Jesuit mission that made life difficult for the Hutterites, and once again recatholization was the goal. For example, a mandate for Sabatisch appeared in 1760, which called for the conversion of the Hutterites to Catholicism. Hutterite elders and preachers who opposed recatholization measures were captured. This time, however, they did not end up in prison, but in monasteries, where they were to be re-educated in Catholic ways; they had to attend Catholic classes and read books about the Catholic faith.[43]

The rest of the community was also subjected to harsh measures similar to those in Transylvania: the Hutterite prayer house was closed and the key given to the Jesuit missionary. The Hutterites had to listen to Catholic sermons and their children were to attend Catholic schools. The sources, however, show that the Hutterites did not accept all of this without resistance and held their services and observed the Lord's Supper in the forest or in private homes. This evasion and all the efforts to continue living the Hutterite faith offered only a short respite. In the end, the attempts at recatholization were increasingly successful. The Hutterite community grew weary and crumbled; members became Catholic. By the mid-1760s at the latest, the Hutterite community in Upper Hungary no longer existed because all remaining Hutterites had converted to Catholicism. However, the sources also say that the Hutterites developed little "Catholic" zeal in the following years.

The Hutterites who had become Catholic are still known today as "Habaner;" their descendants lived in Upper Hungary and Czechoslovakia in the early 20th century.[44] When David Hofer (James Valley, MB) and Michael Waldner (Bon Homme, SD) traveled to Germany in 1937, they also went to Slovakia and visited the Habaner. In Velke Levare they met Joseph Walter, who was the head of the Haban community. He reported that in 1937, 30 families were descendants of the Hutterites; in Sabatisch there were 40 families.

43 von Schlachta, "Gefahr oder Segen?," 389f.
44 Robert Friedmann, "The Habaner," *Hutterite Studies: Celebrating the Life and Work of an Anabaptist Scholar*, 2nd Edition (MacGregor: Hutterian Brethren Book Centre, 2010), 71–73.

David Hofer describes the old *Hof* in Sabatisch in the following way:

> When we entered the village and the car stopped, we were a bit disappointed, not a single Habaner house was to be seen. We went several steps further and soon saw them, the Habaner houses, like the ones in Lewär, situated at the very end of the village. The first thing they showed us was the tower, where the clock and the bells had been stolen from the community during the war. The tower still stands and goes back to our forefathers. On the left side of the tower is the old inn of the Church, on the right side the mill, which still runs daily with two rollers and grinds for the whole village. [...] The cellar, the mill, and the inn are still from our forefathers, and all three are now used jointly by the community. From there we were led to the inn of the Church, where we can see our forefather's beautiful work. There is a beautiful long table made of oak wood, made by the forefathers, which they appreciate and treasure very much. Next to it is a cellar, which is also beautifully decorated, with a small anteroom, so that you don't have to go down into the deep cellar for every little thing.[45]

Hutterites as a Political Issue — Petitions and Denunciations

The attempted recatholization of the Hutterites had a significant political impact. The mandate that Maria Theresa released in 1760 ending toleration of Hutterites initially left a few loopholes. One of them concerned the political attitude of the community. Had the Hutterites recognized that the authorities could be Christians and had they agreed to swear oaths, they could have continued to live undisturbed. Thus, how the Hutterites were positioned politically—whether they recognized the authorities as "Christian," and

---

45 David Hofer, *Reise nach Europa, 1937* (Elie: James Valley Book Centre, 1990), 110.

whether they were politically loyal or would cause unrest or rebellion—was an important question for the Habsburg rulers.

In this situation, the Hutterites decided to write two petitions to Empress Maria Theresa which attempted to present Hutterites as nonthreatening, loyal subjects. These texts offer us an interesting insight into the Hutterite reasoning regarding their own situation.[46] The Hutterites complained about the repressive recatholizing measures which the community faced. They emphasized that they had been living in Upper Hungary for 200 years and had been placed under imperial protection by a privilege of Emperor Leopold I in 1659. They had always lived "peacefully and quietly," paid all the required taxes, and had shown that their way of life was "godly, peaceful, and respectful." They were always loyal to the ruling dynasty. However, none of this was being recognized and taken into account. The Hutterites, according to their petition, were subjected to coercive measures: their leaders were locked up in monasteries and forcibly instructed in the Catholic faith and their children forced to attend a Catholic school. The petitions culminated in a demand to remain with the old Hutterite faith. It was, however, unsuccessful; the situation of the community did not change. The choice was clear: conversion or flight to southern Russia.

But the situation progressed even further in 1781. It was the year when Emperor Joseph II issued several edicts [*Patente*] of tolerance, which, among others, were directed at Protestants. Protestants now received the official concession to publicly practice their faith in the Habsburg countries. Those former Hutterites who still lived in Upper Hungary, in Velke Levare, also tried to take advantage of these toleration edicts. With the publication of the edicts, they began to become politically active and, referring to the tolerance of Protestants, also asked to be allowed to live their old Hutterite faith as well. In fact, something like a spirit of optimism was felt in the Upper Hungarian villages. The former Hutterite Josef Hörndl, a stove builder, ran from house to house with the tolerance edict and encouraged his former brothers and sisters to become Hutterite again.[47]

---

46   The following events from: von Schlachta, "Gefahr oder Segen?," 393–395.
47   von Schlachta, "Gefahr oder Segen?," 395.

In addition, former Hutterites in Upper Hungary made contact with their brothers and sisters in Wischenky. The developing correspondence shows that the Catholicized Hutterites in Upper Hungary no longer expected to find Hutterites in Russia who were actually allowed to practice their faith. Obviously, they had assumed that, like themselves, all Hutterites had been forcibly catholicized. In any case, they were very amazed and delighted when a reply came from Russia and they learned that Hutterites still lived there—that "there was still an authentic community gathered in Russia, which had religious freedom."[48] The Upper Hungarian ex-Hutterites invited their Russian brothers and sisters to visit them and to instruct them in the old orders and traditions so that they would be able to live again in the proper Hutterite way. But they got their hopes up too early, because the ex-Hutterites' awakening was quickly suppressed, nipping all hope in the bud. The authorities made it clear that the tolerance edicts only applied to Protestants and that the Hutterites had to remain Catholic.

The sources provide further details about the life of the former Hutterites at that time. The struggle to return to the Hutterite faith brought to light a deep division among them: not all ex-Hutterites wanted to return to their former faith. Some even saw these efforts as dangerous. They wanted to continue to live quietly and peacefully as "Catholics" and now turned against those who fought for the Hutterite faith. A group including Heinrich Kuen, Tobias Pulmann, Abraham Zeterle, and Johann Amsler stirred up opinion against their politically active former brothers and sisters. They distanced themselves from Hörndl and his people and accused them of wanting to cause unrest. They denounced their former brothers and sisters as "revolutionaries" and "rebels" whose loyalty to the political authorities was seen as questionable.[49]

Interestingly, those Hutterites who wanted to remain Catholic referred to Peter Riedemann's *Rechenschaft* from 1545 and quoted several passages in order to reinforce to what extent Hutterite theology questioned the authorities and how dangerous it ultimately was for political rule. In this way, they wanted to accuse

---
48 Correspondence in: *Chronicle*, vol. 2, 510–517.
49 *Chronicle*, vol. 2, 512f.

their former siblings in faith of being disloyal to the authorities. The quoted passages were taken out of context in such a way that Hutterite theology actually appeared to be particularly open to rebellion and turmoil. In a petition addressed to Joseph II it says:

> Among other misguided articles, we also recognize those of the Anabaptists or Hutterian Brethren as offensive, harmful, and godless. We abhor the following articles: Firstly, that children should not be baptized. Secondly, that no government is considered valid among these Christians. Thirdly, that Christians are not allowed to wage war, neither to pay war taxes, nor to make weapons for that purpose. They clearly and openly teach this in their booklet, entitled: *Confession of our Religion, Teachings, and Faith, by Brothers that one Calls Hutterite, written by Peter Rydemann*, without specifying the place where it was printed.[50]

The ex-Hutterites who campaigned for the Catholic faith also emphasized that they themselves had converted voluntarily and not under pressure, accusing their former siblings of hypocrisy. Jacob Walter, who belonged to the group that wanted to return to the Hutterite faith, directed clear words against his former brothers and sisters. According to him, their former leaders had turned into "the greatest children of Satan" who sought to "suppress the truth and extinguish the light."[51] One way out for those ex-Hutterites who wanted to become Hutterite again was to emigrate to Wischenky. This had to happen secretly. Among those who left Upper Hungary and went to Wischenky were Jacob Walter and his wife as well as Heinrich Wollmann and Heinrich Amsler.

For their part, the Hutterites in Russia made several attempts to help their former brothers and sisters in Upper Hungary. In 1782 they sent two delegations to Vienna to have an audience with Emperor Joseph II. The *Klein-Geschichtbuch* reports quite extensively on these efforts.[52] It reports that four days after the delegation sub-

---

50 Quoted from: von Schlachta, "Gefahr oder Segen?," 396.
51 *Chronicle*, vol. 2, 512.
52 Ibid, 520-523.

mitted their written statement to the court, Hutterite Christian Hofer walked around the Emperor's palace and encountered Emperor Joseph II. The latter asked him to come closer, whereupon the two men spoke to each other for almost half an hour. Joseph is said to have enquired extensively about the Hutterites' origins and beliefs. Christian Hofer, who stemmed from the Carinthian transmigrants, told his story and made his Carinthian origins clear to the emperor. He made the request that the assets and property left behind by the former Protestants during the transmigration should be returned. According to the Hutterite report, Joseph replied that if they would return to their old home, they would get their property back.

The emperor allegedly reacted very incredulously when Hofer explained to him that the Hutterites in Upper Hungary were being persecuted and their elders arrested. The Hutterite chronicler reports:

> At last he [Joseph II] said: 'Yes, what is that? That is a trivial matter; you should profess a religion, whether Catholic, Lutheran, Calvinist or Greek.' The brother replied: 'We don't see a Christian, godly life among them.' The emperor said: 'Oh, you can still be pious and live as you please.' The brother replied: 'We cannot be convinced otherwise in our hearts; for like Christ, the Lord and his apostles teach, one should stick to the pure teaching, follow him and live a Christian, godly life.'[53]

Since nothing had changed in the fate of the ex-Hutterites after their first visit to Vienna, a second delegation consisting of Hutterites from Sabatisch also traveled to Vienna in 1782. They also had direct contact with Joseph II. In a conversation, the emperor was again very open and curious about the Hutterite faith. However, when the request was made to return to the old Hutterite belief, no compromises were possible and Joseph II responded negatively. He made his visitors aware of the advantages of Catholicism and said that child baptism was not "a bad thing" and that there was

---

53   Ibid, 515.

no need to worship images. He himself was a Catholic and also did not worship an image. The Hutterites should follow his example and stay with the faith where "the head is, by which he meant himself, or profess the Lutheran, Calvinist, or Greek religion."[54]

Opportunity for Reflection
How was history used as an argument in the various crises that the Hutterite Church went through? What is the significance of politics for Hutterites today?

---

54   Ibid, 522.

LECTURE FOUR
"We do not wish nor desire to do harm or evil to any man."[1]

Johannes Waldner passed away in 1824. He stands in the company of the more prominent Hutterite *Ältesten*, specifically representing the emigration of the Hutterites from Transylvania and the transition of the community into the 19th century. When the community set out in 1767 to leave Alwinz, Kreuz, and Stein, they left behind the lands and authority of the Habsburgs and came into the territory and under the authority of the Russian tsars. The Hutterites, however, did not initially settle on crown land, i.e., on the land of the tsar, but on the property of Count Peter Rumyantsev-Zadunaisky. This small-but-significant difference became consequential around 1800 when the old count died and his heirs no longer wanted to grant the Hutterites all the privileges they had received when they settled in Wischenky. In 1802, Johannes Waldner led the Hutterites from Wischenky to Radiceva.

Defencelessness was an essential point in the dispute with the heirs of Count Rumyantsev-Zadunaisky.[2] The new owner of Wischenky, Count Sergej Petrowitz von Rumyantsev, did not want to grant this to the Hutterites, but demanded that they serve as soldiers in the event of a war. The male parishioners were registered and had to pay a bounty if they wanted to buy their way out of military service. The Mennonites, who at that time were already settling on the crown property of the Russian tsar in southern Russia, had been granted exactly those privileges for which the Hutterites were fight-

---

1 *Chronicle*, vol. 1, 112.
2 *Chronicle*, vol. 2, 568f.

ing and did not have to participate in military service. The Hutterites recognized this as an opportunity and, in the subsequent negotiations with the Russian authorities, specifically emphasized that the Mennonites were their "closest relatives in faith" and that their privileges should therefore also apply to the Hutterites.[3] Johannes Waldner and Christian Hofer traveled to St. Petersburg in 1797 to negotiate the political framework for Hutterite life. They spoke to Count Rumyantsev-Zadunaisky and submitted a petition to Tsar Paul I in which they demanded the same privileges the Mennonites had. Their efforts were initially unsuccessful.

The Hutterites, however, persisted. After the death of Paul I, they interceded with his successor, Tsar Alexander I, who took power in 1801. They asked again for the right to leave Count Rumyantsev-Zadunaisky's lands and settle on crown land. The political conditions were now obviously more favourable, because a short time later, in May of the same year, the application was successful and Hutterites were given permission to settle on crown land. The ministerial order of May 22, 1801 was the 'door opener' for settlement in Radiceva. Interestingly enough, the Tsar's decree also lables Hutterites as 'Mennonites,' which indicates once again that Hutterites presented themselves as 'Mennonites' in the political negotiations. This politically motivated argument worked well, but reveals little about actual confessional identification. We know from other sources that the Hutterites didn't really want to associate too closely with Mennonites. The very heated discussions between Hutterites and Mennonites in West Prussia had taken place less than 20 years earlier. Almost at the same time, Johannes Waldner denied having a close relationship with the Mennonites in his correspondence with the Moravian Brethren pastor, Johann Wiegand. Still, the ministerial order stated that the petition should be granted:

> Mennonites settled in the Little Russian Gouvernement in Wischenka, an estate belonging to Count Sergei Rumyantsev, a member of the Secret Council [*Wirklichen Geheimen Rate*], and requesting transfer to crown land to be leased by them and given similar privileges as the Russian Mennonites.[4]

---

3   Ibid, 572f, 575.
4   Ibid, 575f.

Thus, after 1801 the Hutterites were 'free imperial people' and direct subjects of the Russian crown, which they remained after moving to the Molotschna in 1842. Their military registration [*Einschreibung in die Revision*] was cancelled, which means their privilege not to participate in military service was reinstated. The community did not have to move very far in 1802, because a year earlier they had leased some properties on nearby crown land, which they could now settle. The wooden houses in Wischenky could be dismantled and rebuilt in Radiceva.

Defencelessness was always granted as a privilege to both Hutterites and Mennonites in the Early Modern period. They did not have to perform military service and were protected by exceptional provisions. This was more or less a 'bonus' for the settlement on the various estates. Thus, for most of their history, defencelessness in terms of taking up arms in times of war was not a matter of conscience for the Hutterites, because it was legally guaranteed they would not have to take up arms. Defencelessness only had to be negotiated again in times of distress, when estates changed hands or when it was necessary to migrate and find a new home.

In 1842 the Hutterites finally moved to the Molotschna and were confronted with political questions in a completely new way, as described in the last lecture. For the first time the topic of political participation was so present and pressing that it led to conflicts within the community. The Hutterites had become part of the regional self-government granted to the Mennonites. This not only meant that Hutterites had to provide a *Schulze* and two assessors, but also that defencelessness now became a topic requiring discussion. And not only with respect to the question of whether one should take up arms and go to war or not, but also according to the motto that was chosen as the title for this lecture: "We do not wish nor desire to do harm or evil to any man." In the Anabaptist understanding, defencelessness was always more than military service—it was an entire way of life in a holistic sense.

But first, an overview of the position of the Hutterites towards defencelessness and political authority throughout their history is required as background.

Theological Justifications for Defencelessness

It is often said in broad sweeping terms that, because Anabaptists did not go to war, they translated the message of the Decalogue, "You shall not kill," into practical life in a consistent manner. This simple and unambiguous statement is indeed an essential aspect of defencelessness, but defencelessness encompasses even more; for the Hutterites, as for all other Anabaptists, it was much more complex. First of all, it was always a holistic question relating to interpersonal relationships: How do I deal with my neighbour? Secondly, the question of defencelessness in Anabaptist theology cannot be considered without examining their stance towards politics and the authorities because the theological justifications are too closely linked.

As early as the 16th century, defencelessness meant more to the Anabaptists than deciding whether to go to war or not. In regard to the term, Anabaptist defencelessness was thus always more than political 'pacifism,' as it is now often described in a very generalized way. 'Pacifism' is a term from international law, and as a word and phenomenon, only an achievement of the early 20th century. It described forms of conflict settlement between individual states based on the premise of establishing peace—this was the objective of the peace movement, which was still very young around 1900. That the Anabaptist understanding of defencelessness was more than 'political pacifism' becomes clear when one looks at the relevant texts in the foundational writings of the Hutterites, for example, Riedemann's *Rechenschaft* or the *Five Articles* published in the 1570s, under the heading, "Christians may not wage war, administer worldly law, or use force and the sword. People in these positions cannot be considered Christians," the *Five Articles*, as printed in the Hutterite *Geschichtbuch* under the year 1547, state:

> Jacob the patriarch prophesied that the sceptre should pass from Judah at the coming of the victor, who is Christ. Since the ruling power of the Jews (the people of God in those days) came to an end in Christ and was taken from them, it is plain that in Christ it should have no existence and that from now on the new people of God should not carry

or use the worldly sword or rule by it. Christ alone will rule his people, governing them with the sword of his spirit.[5]

The *Five Articles* briefly repeat what Peter Riedemann wrote about defencelessness in his *Rechenschaft*. Riedemann traced the separation of the kingdoms to the transition from the Old to the New Testament. With the coming of Jesus Christ, the 'Jewish rule' had ended and the 'sceptre of Judah' was taken away; the kingdom of Christ had appeared. In this new kingdom, which continues with Christianity, Jesus Christ does not rule with the 'worldly sword,' like the Jews in the Old Testament, but with the 'spiritual sword.' This periodization provides Riedemann with the justification that in the New Testament kingdom of Christ the secular sword no longer has any power or legitimation. And this is exactly where the sharp division between the kingdoms made by the Hutterites begins. "The sword of the Spirit and the sword of this world each has its own sheath."[6]

In the 'world' there are "beating, stabbing, shooting, and injuring one another; destroying, quarrelling, killing, and bloodshed, there is the devil's ungodly mountain, the abode of Lucifer."[7] In contrast, other values are valid in God's kingdom, for example the following found in Matthew 5 and quoted by the Hutterites: "Blessed are the meek. Blessed are the merciful. Blessed are the peacemakers. Blessed are those who are persecuted for the sake of righteousness." Thus, a church that takes following Jesus Christ seriously cannot exist within this world or be associated with it because the basic norms are completely different. For the Hutterites it follows that a Christian cannot assume any office in government, because no government can satisfy Christian norms. Meekness, mercy, and peaceableness, says the *Geschichtbuch*, is "in every way contrary to the office of the sword and violence." And to refer once again to a statement found in the *Five Articles*: Jesus Christ "never entrusted the power of the sword to any apostle or disciple in his church."[8]

---

5   *Chronicle*, vol. 1, 276.
6   Peter Riedemann, *Rechenschaft*, 102–105.
7   *Chronicle*, vol. 1, 278.
8   Ibid, 228, 280.

In addition, the 'world' did not tolerate the Anabaptists' standards—the Hutterites had experienced this firsthand. However, like Anabaptists in general, Hutterites did not deny the legitimacy of the authorities per se. On the contrary, they were convinced that the authorities lawfully exercised violence and used the sword in a legitimate manner. Indeed, they must use it, because it is their role to protect the good and punish the bad, that is, to administer justice. In the Hutterite conception, the government office was instituted by God, and it remained divinely instituted, even if the holders of the offices exercised them poorly and not according to God's intent. For the Hutterites it was fundamental that God had ordained the authorities to protect the good and punish the bad. Therefore, according to Anabaptist beliefs, resistance was not an option because it would have called God's order into question.

This sharp separation of the secular from the spiritual kingdom and the simultaneous recognition of the order-creating task of the authorities are also attested by the Schleitheim Articles, which in 1527 represented an attempt to give the very diverse early Anabaptist movement a normative guideline. One of its statements was taken up by the Hutterite *Geschichtbuch*:

> The sword is an order of God outside the perfection of Christ. It punishes the bad and protects and shields the good. In the law, the sword is ordained over the wicked as punishment and death. The worldly authorities are appointed to use it. In the perfection of Christ, however, the ban is only used to admonish and exclude those who have sinned, not by killing the flesh, but solely by warning and the command not to sin anymore.[9]

The Hutterites draw on the statements of the Schleitheim Articles in their "Description of the Community" appearing under the year 1569 in the *Große Geschichtbuch*.

Because the use of the sword is an ordinance of God outside the kingdom of Christ, the authorities should have no power in the

---

9   Quoted from: Urs B. Leu and Christian Scheidegger, eds., *Das Schleitheimer Bekenntnis 1527* (Zug: Achius Verlag, 2004), 69.

church, and vice versa, no Christian should hold an office in government. This conviction, or rather the turning away from it, formed the basis for all discussions Hutterites had in the Molotschna about the legitimacy and competencies of the office of the *Schulze*. The *Schulze* was a Hutterite, but at the same time represented the secular and worldly authorities and thus also had the right to pronounce justice within the community. At the same time, he was legitimized to use force and to execute punishments prescribed by the Russian legal system. This shifted the question of defencelessness away from waging war and 'taking up arms' on the Hutterite agenda.

If one surveys Anabaptist history, it becomes clear that 'defencelessness' was not always seen and interpreted uniformly in the various Anabaptist traditions. This reveals once again that it is impossible to speak of a single Anabaptist theology. Just as there was no such thing as 'the' Anabaptists as a homogeneous group, 'one' attitude to defencelessness and to the political authorities cannot be found.

Hutterites, as we have seen, believed that a Christian must live strictly defenceless. From this it followed for them that Christians should not defend themselves, even in personal conflict, but must rather live peacefully with other humans. A Christian should not pay war taxes and should not assume any office in government, such as that of a *Schulze* or city council. Politics can never be Christian according to the Hutterites, because Christian norms could never be implemented politically. According to the Hutterite view, this meant that if a Christian was politically active, he would never be able to follow his conscience—politics inevitably corrupt.

Other Anabaptists, such as Balthasar Hubmaier, who was active in Nikolsburg in the late 1520s, were not as strict on these issues. Hubmaier said that politics could well be shaped according to Christian standards, and thus he was also convinced that a Christian could assume a government office.[10] This raised the question of violence, which Hubmaier answered politically. He allowed a Christian who had an official position to use violence if this served to restore order in society according to God's ordinances, i.e., to help the authorities in fulfilling this task, for example to take up

---

10 von Schlachta, *Täufer*, 131–138.

arms when the draft is invoked. However, one should consider the motives. According to Hubmaier, one should "test the spirit" of the authorities "to see whether they are motivated more by arrogance, pride, greed, hate, or their own benefit instead of love for the common good and the wellbeing of the country." Thus, according to the divine order, the government did not wield the sword, "for sabre-rattling, or to wage war, attack, assault, fly off the handle, fight, and tyrannize," but rather to protect orphans and widows, to lead the pious, and to free all those who are coerced and oppressed by violence. It is a fundamental duty of Christians to pray for a pious, just and Christian government so that one could lead a peaceful and quiet life in godliness and honesty.[11]

Menno Simons, the namesake of the Mennonites, also took a nuanced view. He spoke out against waging war and in favour of a peaceful life. True Christians, according to Menno Simons, had forged their swords into ploughshares and made their spears into sickles. For him this does not mean seeking "money, goods, destruction or blood," but "the honour and praise of their God and the salvation of our souls." Christians are "children of peace," whose hearts overflow with peace, whose mouth speaks of peace and who walk on the path of peace. Instead of calling for vengeance, they would pray with Jesus Christ: "Father, forgive them; for they do not know what they are doing."[12]

At the same time, however, Menno Simons displayed a good deal of pragmatism. He recognized that there were also 'good authorities,' but that they were 'very small' in number. The "Wismar Articles," which Menno Simons wrote together with other preachers in 1554, contain the following instruction:

> If a believer shouldered a stick or rapier on the road according to the custom of the country, the elders cannot consider it improper. But the elders do not consider it right that a Christian should present or

---

11 Gunnar Westin and Torsten Bergsten, eds., *Balthasar Hubmaier: Schriften*, Quellen zur Geschichte der Täufer, vol. 9 (Gütersloh: C. Bertelsmann, 1962), 443, 454f.
12 Menno Simons, *Die Schriften des Menno Simons: Gesamtausgabe* (Weierhof: Mennonitische Forschungsstelle/Steinhagen: Samenkorn, 2013), 607f.

> use weapons for defence in response to orders from the authorities, unless he is a soldier.[13]

This instruction can be interpreted to mean that the Anabaptists should oppose conscription, but employment as a soldier was conceivable.

In connection with the subject of 'defencelessness' the question must also be asked what ideas the Anabaptists had about the order and functioning of society. Is defencelessness a realistic option for society as a whole or is it just a utopia to be pursued? Indeed, the sources show that the Anabaptists were confronted by such questions. In 1577, Peter Walpot responded to these challenges directed at the Hutterites in the Great Article Book [*Großen Artikelbuch*]: "If we all renounced the sword and did as you do and say, who would resist the Turks and the enemy?" Walpot replied to this criticism: "If we were all Christians, God would resist the enemy. For he alone is the protector of his little flock."[14]

So, the Anabaptists of the 16th century had their thoughts about war and peace and about the organization of society and the enforcement of law and order. However, the ongoing reality of persecution ensured that they themselves could not actively engage in society. In addition, defencelessness affected other areas of Anabaptist life, such as the question of whether vengeance is allowed. The "Description of the Community" in the *große Geschichtbuch* paints a picture of a Hutterite community in which there was neither war, nor vengeance, nor war taxes:

> Swords and spears were forged into pruning knives, scythes and other tools. There was no musket, sabre, halberd, or any weapon of defence. Each was a brother to the other. They were a thoroughly peaceful people who never took part in any war or bloodshed by paying war taxes, much less by active participation. They did not resort to revenge—patience was their weapon in all conflict.[15]

---

13   Ibid, 222, 940.
14   Quoted from: Ernst Laubach, "'kain obrigkait zu erkhennen und sich dem Turkhen angengig zu machen…:' Zu einer Stigmatisierung der Täufer im 16. Jahrhundert," *Zeitschrift für Historische Forschung* 37 (2010): 431.
15   *Chronicle*, vol. 1, 404.

"Holding Fast to What is Good?"

This specified how one should treat personal conflicts: by being nonviolent and pursuing peace! Do not resist, but remain calm [*stillhalten*] and use patience as a weapon! Endure injustice, as it says in Matthew 5:39: "But I say to you, do not resist an evildoer. But if anyone strikes you on the right cheek, turn the other also; and if anyone wants to sue you and take your coat, give your cloak as well." So how does an Anabaptist react when his own *Hof* is being attacked? What do you do when the rulers' henchmen persecute religious refugees?

And how did an Anabaptist travel? Perhaps an unusual question, but it also concerned defencelessness, because traveling was a dangerous activity in the 16th century. Robbers were waiting everywhere, and so Anabaptists had to make a decision as to whether or not to resist an attack. Usually one had a walking stick on a journey, because it made walking more comfortable, but could also be used to repel robbers in the event of an attack. In other words, it could also be used as a weapon. Menno Simons, as already quoted, allowed his followers to arm themselves when travelling. Similar statements are handed down from the Tyrol and Saxony, where Anabaptists only carried a stick with them, but no rapier or sword. In 1532, during the interrogation of Sigmund from Kiens, it was said that the leaders would forbid them to "carry anything other than a stick;" in Saxony there is talk of a "small stick [*Stäblein*]." However, one ought not to defend oneself during capture. Hans Grembser, an Anabaptist from the Pustertal, also testified in 1533 that Anabaptists could be recognized by the fact that they carried no weapons.[16] The historian of the Swiss town of St. Gallen, Johannes Kessler, stated in his book Sabbata that the Anabaptists would forgo any form of protection on their travels and that apart from a "broken bread knife" they would carry neither sword nor rapier with them.[17]

---

16   Grete Mecenseffy and Matthias Schmelzer, eds., *Österreich, 3. Teil*, Quellen zur Geschichte der Täufer, vol. 14, (Heidelberg: Verein für Reformationsgeschichte, 1983), 21; Paul Wappler, "Die Stellung Kursachsens und des Landgrafen Philipp von Hessen zur Täuferbewegung," *Reformationsgeschichtliche Studien und Texte* 13 and 14, (1910): 140.

17   Emil Egli and Rudolf Schoch, eds., *Johann Keßler's Sabbata mit kleinen Schriften und Briefen*, (St. Gallen, 1902), 147.

There are ongoing debates about the meaning of a passage in the sources concerning Jakob Huter. It states that Huter had a *hackl* in his arm; some sources even talk of a rifle. Historians are still not quite sure what to make of this description of Jakob Huter. Had Huter really armed himself for his numerous journeys, as was quite common in the Early Modern period? Or are these statements perhaps just a polemical denigration of the Anabaptist preacher by his opponents? Or does *hackl* just mean a narrow axe, a meaning that the word also had in the 16th century? The latter is likely.[18]

Defencelessness in Hutterite History

Defencelessness played an essential role in the beginnings of the Hutterite community and for the Anabaptists associated with Jakob Wiedemann who moved out of Nikolsburg in 1528. This group of Anabaptists had come into conflict with Balthasar Hubmaier, among other matters, over the question of attitude towards authorities, in which Hubmaier, as we have seen, took a very open position. He did not make as sharp a distinction between the Anabaptist communities and the political sphere as the later Hutterites. The group around Jakob Wiedemann, on the other hand, held ideas of strict defencelessness, and so conflicts with Hubmaier, but also with the Lords of Nikolsburg—the Lords of Liechtenstein—soon developed. The Hutterite *Geschichtbuch* reports that the Nikolsburgers rejected the strict form of defencelessness and preached against it. The corresponding labels were quickly established: everyone who adhered to the idea of defencelessness was nicknamed *Stäbler*, and those who allowed Christians to use the sword were called *Schwertler*.

As landlords of the region, the Lords of Liechtenstein refused the *Stäbler* permanent settlement and drove them out again, so they moved to the Austerlitz area. The group led by Jakob Wiedemann obviously had been quite destitute and perhaps even came to Moravia largely penniless. The displaced people saw the way out of this predicament by pooling everything they had. The Hutterite *Geschichtbuch* reports that on the road between Tannewitz and Muschau, Wiedemann and his people spread a coat on which

---

18 Grete Mecenseffy and Matthias Schmelzer, eds., *Österreich, 3. Teil*, 37; Packull, *Hutterite Beginnings*, 174f.

everyone placed their property—community-of-goods was established, and the Hutterites came into being.[19] This is the story of the founding of the Hutterites, a story accompanied by the desire for a life of pursuing peace and nonviolence.

The question of whether and how to react to violence arose again and again for the Hutterites during the Turkish wars of the early 17th century. It was a very hard time because the Turkish wars caused considerable suffering on the Hutterite communities; assaults by marauding troops were common. The Hutterite *Geschichtbuch*, for example, writes for the year 1605:

> [...] the Lord's community [has] suffered immeasurable damage this year, with the enemy (as reported) burning, robbing, murdering and capturing people, and [the community] also experienced loss and endured a lot of stress and hardship through the soldiers who were in the country for a long time.[20]

During these times the question of to what extent one can resist attacks in order to defend one's community and people repeatedly arose, because the Hutterite *Bruderhöfe* suffered not only material damage that at the hands of the various troops, but also lost members. This is tragically reflected in the events surrounding Salomon Böger, the Hutterite who traveled to Constantinople to ransom and free captured and enslaved Hutterites.

It seems that Hutterites did not give up defencelessness in the 18th century either. In 1750 the community came into closer contact with the Mennonites in the Netherlands. It was the time when infant baptism had actually already been introduced in Upper Hungary, where Zacharias Walter was the elder. In other words, it was the time when the authorities pressured the Hutterites to practice infant baptism. Community-of-property had also been given up. In the course of ongoing correspondence, the elder Zacharias Walter sent the Mennonites a creed of the Hutterites, which also dealt with defencelessness. According to Walter, the Hutter-

---

19   *Chronicle*, vol. 1, 80f; Packull, *Hutterite Beginnings*, 61–66.
20   *Chronicle*, vol. 1, 584.

ites continued to practice this. The church used neither sword nor vengeance, because in the Bible it says, "Revenge is mine, says the Lord."[21] One should not resist evil with evil, but rather, love one's enemies and pray for them.[22]

Hutterite history also contains episodes that show that the theory and practice of defencelessness were two different things. For example, the *Klein-Geschichtbuch* provides a report of a community meeting in Velke Levare in 1633. One of the issues under discussion was how to deal with violence. It says that some

> brothers resisted the magistrates, their attendants, and similar people by rushing together to defend themselves with blows and a great show of violence As a result we not only have a sin against God on our consciences but have also made ourselves liable to the utmost penalty of the law and have caused the highest authorities in the land to regard us as inso lent, rebellious people and arrogant scoundrels.[23]

We have seen how the question of defencelessness in the Early Modern period cannot be considered without taking into account the historic positioning of the Anabaptists in relation to society as a whole and to authorities. But how can one define a position in relation to an authority that enforces its authority and power so rigorously that it persecutes those with a different faith? To an authority that wages war and executes death sentences—in Hutterite terms, "does the complete opposite" of what the New Testament demands? How does one classify such an authority? In extreme cases, such discussions involve the question of resistance and civil disobedience. Besides these social and political questions, however, all aspects of defencelessness should extend into the personal area—defencelessness must be a way of life in the holistic sense.

---

21 Deuteronomy 32:35; Romans 12:19.
22 von Schlachta, "*Als ob man uns von engeln gottes saget*," 218f.
23 *Chronicle*, vol. 2, 226f.

The 19th Century and the Question of Defencelessness as a Touchstone for Anabaptist Communities

As indicated, Anabaptist congregations found different answers to the question of violence, and numerous compromises were made as early as the Early Modern period. It is known that, beginning in the early 17th century, members of the Mennonites mainly from municipalities such as Krefeld or Friedrichstadt, served as mayors or members of the city council. Three Mennonite representatives were also part of the Paulskirche parliament in Frankfurt am Main in 1848, which debated, among other things, whether the various German territories could be united into one state and how one should meet the revolutionaries' demands for democracy. From the late 18th century onwards, members of Mennonite communities had gone to war; for example, they had taken part in the Wars of Liberation in the Netherlands and the Napoleonic Wars. Mennonites also appeared as soldiers in the wars of 1870–71, during the unification of Germany—and finally, participated in the First and Second World Wars.[24]

All Anabaptist congregations were affected by the fundamental political changes that were taking place in the 19th century. These changes were connected with the realization of new ideas: the implementation of human rights and the desire to guarantee equal rights for all citizens. Conversely, however, this means that where everyone is equal, there can be no legal privileges or exceptions. As a result, in the 19th century Anabaptist communities lost their privilege of being exempt from military service. Often, however, the Mennonites were able to fight for some exceptions. In 1868, a cabinet order issued by the Prussian King granted the Mennonites permission to do medical and supply services, and the Russian Mennonites were allowed to do forestry services.

Acculturation began in many Anabaptist communities in the 19th century. The Anabaptists became part of society and the distance to the 'world' or separation weakened. This integration into society prepared many Anabaptists to approach society on their own initiative and to demonstrate a decreased will to refuse military

---
24 von Schlachta, *Täufer*, 242f.

service. In the USA and Canada, too, the Mennonites lost some of their reservations about military service. Mennonites already fought in the Civil War, while at the same time other Mennonites campaigned for a general exemption from military service and for the legal status of a conscientious objector. The political question thus created tensions among the various Anabaptist groups.

As far as can be seen from the sources, some Hutterites gave up their reservations about military service only in the First World War. The community in Radiceva and the Molotchna had been assured the privilege of not having to participate in armed conflicts. Thus, within the community the debates about the use of force remained focused on those conflicts and discussions already described, which revolved around the influence of the Mennonites and the *Schulzenamt*. It was not until the second half of the 19th century that the question of bearing arms and military service came back on the agenda. Beginning in the mid-1850s, the general situation of the settlers in southern Russia deteriorated as they gradually lost their privileges and rights of self-government. There were rumours that the German colonies should be Russified, which would have meant the introduction of the Russian language in the Hutterite and Mennonite schools, as well as the general strengthening of Russian culture in various areas of life. In addition, there was a threat of losing the privilege of not having to do military service.[25]

A group of Hutterites and Mennonites began thinking about alternative settlement options as early as the early 1870s. In 1872 the first Mennonite delegation went to North America to investigate the situation there. A year later, a second delegation followed, in which two Hutterite preachers, Paul and Lorenz Tschetter from Neu-Hutterthal, also participated. Their feedback was positive and, in the course of the 1870s, 1,250 Hutterites finally emigrated to the USA.

The Question of Defencelessness in World War I

Until the First World War, the right to refuse military service as a conscientious objector was not legally enshrined or stipulated by law. It was also not a constitutional right, but rather the release

---

25   von Schlachta, *From the Tyrol to North America*, 156–162.

from bearing arms could be granted on humanitarian grounds or as a one-time privilege, depending on the situation. The discussions concerning conscientious objectors continued during the First World War. The Quakers were leaders in asking for exceptions for the Peace Churches; very early on they lobbied Washington in a highly organized manner to contend for the possibility of conscientious objection to military service.

The Hutterites were still critical of military service during this time, but registered their young people in the hope they would not be drafted as an act of goodwill towards the authorities. Ultimately, however, President Wilson determined that there would be no exceptions. Everyone would have to do military service, but Wilson granted the option of doing non-military alternative service, which, however, also entailed wearing a uniform. There was no alternative service outside the army. This particularly affected the Hutterites, who generally refused to wear a uniform as well as any kind of alternative service, such as in medical or supply units.

This arrangement resulted in much suffering and torture for those registered Hutterites who were drafted but steadfastly refused to wear uniforms and drill. They were tortured, walked the gauntlet, and ended up in prison. In the summer of 1918 the brothers David, Joseph, and Michael Hofer and Jacob Wipf had to answer before a court. Some passages from the interrogations of the Hutterites are very revealing with regard to the Hutterite attitude. Jacob Wipf was asked:

> "Now, what are the principles of your religious organization as they have existed from the beginning? That is, with regard to participation in war? [...] Are the members of your church permitted by your church principles to engage in war?"
> And he replied: "They are strictly against war. That is why we left Russia."

In addition, the American judges tried to find out the national self-definition of the Hutterites, because another question was, "Are you loyal to Germany?"

Wipf replied, "No," and when asked why the Hutterites continue to speak German, he said:

> Well, they started in Germany, and they just kept going as a colony and always kept talking like this. But my father can speak the Russian language. But, we have never gotten out in the world, and just kept that language because they started in Germany.[26]

Then the judges asked more deeply about the defencelessness of the Hutterites:

> "Does your religion believe in fighting of any kind?"
> "No," Wipf answered.
> "You would not fight with your fists?"
> "Well, we ain't no angels. Little boys will scrap sometimes, and we are punished; but our religion don't allow it."
> Finally came the question: "To put the case like this: If a man was attacking or assaulting your sister, would you fight?"
> "No," Wipf answered once again.
> "Would you kill him?"
> "No."
> "What would you do?"
> "Well, in a way, if I could get her away, I might hold him. If I was man enough, I would do that. If I couldn't, I would have to let go. We can't kill. That is strictly against our religion."[27]

Joseph Hofer answered the question why he could not take part in the war in the following way: "Christ says that you shall not kill. We confessed that this is right, and my conscience tells me that."[28]

But not all Hutterites would have agreed with these answers from the Hofer brothers and Jacob Wipf during the First World War.

---

26 Duane C.S. Stotzfus, *Pacifists in Chains: The Persecution of Hutterites during the Great War* (Baltimore: John Hopkins University Press, 2013), 84f; Patrick Murphy et al, *Hutterite COs in World War One: Stories, Diaries, and other Accounts from the United States Military Camps*, 2nd Ed (Hawley: Spring Prairie Printing, 1999).
27 Stoltzfus, *Pacifists in Chains*, 86.
28 Stoltzfus, *Pacifists in Chains*, 88.

World War I was the first time Hutterites went to war—an example is a Hutterite from Wolf Creek, SD. They went to France with the American troops and one of the Hutterite soldiers did not return: he was killed in action in October 1918 and is buried in France.

Opportunity for Reflection
What was the significance of defencelessness in Hutterite history? What do we mean by 'defencelessness' today?

CONCLUSION
500 Years of Hutterite History: A Story of Vibrancy, Rigidity, Change, and the Need to Test all Things

The Hutterites proved to be a dynamic and ever-expanding Anabaptist community in the 16th century. Due to the continuing mission activities of the *Sendboten* and the resulting immigration, the Hutterite *Haushaben* increased in number. Until its expulsion from Moravia, the Hutterite church also developed into a very successful economic enterprise. The Hutterites fitted ideally into the economy of the noble estates in Moravia and served a far-reaching market with their handicraft products.

However, all these developments did not always have a good effect on the confessional situation within the community. It is true that, compared to other Anabaptist congregations, the Hutterites produced a very comprehensive, detailed confessional literature that addressed many issues. Many ordinances regulated social, economic, and confessional interaction in the congregation in a very exhaustive manner. However, the commitment of all members of the congregation to common rules and norms proved to be extremely difficult to achieve. Deviance from the norm appears to have been the order of the day, especially in regard to the idea of community-of-goods: self-interest, individualization, and "disorder" characterized many areas of communal life. The elders tried to counteract this trend by enacting new regulations. However, each new regulation made the community more rigid and decreased potential for dynamism and liveliness.

Precisely these developments ran their course in the Hutterite community until the beginning of the 17th century. The Hutterite elders attempted to eliminate problems by means of new *Ordnungen*, which resulted in more inflexibility and an even greater rigidity. This brought the idea of renewal back in focus again and again. It was thus natural that Hutterite members regularly expressed a desire for spiritual renewal and vitality, something that is necessary in every church.

During the 17th and 18th centuries Hutterites were actively struggling to find the right way, a way between the traditions and rules they had inherited, and the adaptation of these rules to ever-changing conditions. The close communal life of the Hutterites presented the unique challenge of balancing the spiritual and material dimensions, or the communal and the individual realms. Especially instructive in this regard is a formulation in a letter the Hutterites sent to the Mennonites in 1665, where it states that they strove to "establish a *Gemeinschaft* in true Christian form, and in both spiritual and material aspects to aim for perfection and to actually put it into practice."[1]

In the end, the fact that the Hutterites had an enormous collection of old books, confessions of faith, letters, homilies, songs, and *Ordnungen* at their disposal was both positive and negative. On the one hand, the old texts provided the base on which the community could reorganize itself following a crisis. They were responsible for the fact that the community could survive for nearly 500 years. The Hutterites were always able to reorganize their shared life after a crisis. On the other hand, always referring back to the old texts can also hinder renewal and harbours the danger of reimposing historical structures 1:1 in a different era without having tested whether it is still relevant. The art of dealing with traditions, rules, and norms consists in continually putting them to a spiritual test, to not simply throw them overboard in the process, but neither to completely submit to them. Every church community needs regular renewal. The old writings, the stories and the inherited norms can become guidelines for current times and accompany renewal when they don't force communities into an inflexible system, but

---

1 *Das große Geschichtbuch der Hutterischen Brüder*, 668–669.

instead are thoughtfully incorporated into the confessional heritage. To deal wisely with history means to be mentally flexible, to test everything, and to keep what is good.

"Test everything and hold fast to what is good." This phrase from 1 Thessalonian 5 is not only relavant to the cross-confessional contacts and exchanges of Hutterites in the 18th century. Johannes Waldner used it in relation to the *Ordnungen* of his own Hutterite community, as is evident in the following reflection in the *Klein-Geschichtsbuch*:

> After brother Hans Kleinsasser had died and Mathies Hofer had left the community, the order of worship they had introduced began little by little to lapse and disappear. I do not mean to commend this neglect, nor am I glad for it. The gatherings for prayer and especially the reading at midday helped build up the young people's faith. As previously described, each read in turn and so each was involved, and it often led to a talk about the meaning of a passage of the Bible. At that time each one took pains to be able to read out the Scripture fluently, and such a practice should still be used with a good conscience today. Now each young brothers wants to have a good, well-bound Bible with big print, but many of them (always excepting the zealous) know little of what is inside. Paul taught in 1 Thessalonians 5:2, "Prove all things, hold fast to that which is good." It would have been possible to drop what was unnecessary and exaggerated and to keep what was good. But each can judge the matter as he sees fit.[2]

Over and over, the observance of community-of-goods became the centre of Hutterite faith. In this regard I once heard the following observation during a visit to a Hutterite community: In Hutterite history, the wagon was often placed before the horse. Yet the proper order must be: The horse (Jesus Christ) pulling the

---

2 *Chronicle*, vol. 2, 504–505.

wagon (community-of-goods). *Gütergemeinschaft* should not be a system of coercion, but should be lived freely and willingly—with *Freiwilligkeit und Gelassenheit*. The community members must be mature Christians who are aware that discipleship is costly and can assume responsibility for themselves and for others.

In Luke 14:33–35 we read:

> So therefore, none of you can become my disciple if you do not give up all your possessions. Salt is good; but if salt has lost its taste, how can its saltiness be restored? It is fit neither for the soil nor for the manure pile; they throw it away. Let anyone with ears to hear listen!

"Sell everything, for I will care for you"—so says Jesus Christ to his disciples. "The community cares for you," say the Hutterites, "but it costs something." Is it true that, "It is only with good order that something can endure…"? Yes, but good order must never determine faith, but can only support it. It should assist in living out faith, but not be a substitute for faith. When regulations determine faith, they cause faith to become stifling. For that reason, ordinances must constantly be re-evaluated: do they still serve the community well and do they still fit current developments, conditions and challenges? Are they merely oppressive or can they be lived freely? Only then can something endure—in good order!

About Jacob D. Maendel (1911–1972)

Jacob D. Maendel was a Hutterite teacher, pastor, and community leader. Born in 1911 at Rosedale Community near Alexandria, South Dakota, he migrated to Manitoba in 1918 when Hutterites fled political persecution because of their commitment to nonviolence. He was chosen as minister in 1949 at New Rosedale Community and went on to become widely regarded as a leader ahead of his time.

In an era when it was considered good economic sense to clear wooded land for use as fertile farmland, he insisted that strips of forest be conserved as ecological buffer zones. Both the task of selecting the site for a new community and the work of establishing Fairholme Community (1957–1959) were informed by his deep appreciation for nature: Jacob insisted on an acreage of bush above the Assiniboine River, and ensured that the natural environment remains as intact as possible, thereby gaining a reputation as "a staunch defender of trees."

Jacob Maendel also had an ecumenical vision. Although Hutterites of the mid-20th century were characterized by exclusivism and sectarianism, Jacob was open to learning from non-Hutterites in a way that was enriching for the larger Hutterian Community. His outward-looking vision of faithful Christian discipleship led to newcomers—families as well as single adults—visiting New Rosedale: some stayed briefly, while others became permanent members.

Despite his basic grade seven education, he was a self-educated lifelong learner who read widely and introduced his students to great thinkers like Dietrich Bonhoeffer, Sigmund Freud, Helen Keller, and John Milton. Maendel understood the value of a culturally sensitive education and his vision led to the teaching career of Peter Maendel—the first Hutterite to attend and graduate from the Manitoba Teacher's College. This resulted in the unique dynasty of Maendel educators among Manitoba Hutterites today.

Ultimately, Jacob's vision and focus were the impetus for a surge of interest in education among Schmiedeleut I Hutterites that has culminated in nearly 100 Hutterite teachers holding Arts and Education degrees and teaching Hutterite children in their respective communities.

Jacob Maendel died in 1972. With gratitude to God for his work, witness, and inspiration, we name this lecture series in his honour.

About Astrid von Schlachta

Astrid von Schlachta is the historian and director of the Mennonitische Forschungsstelle [Mennonite Research Centre] in Weierhof, Germany; lecturer at the University of Regensburg. For nearly her entire academic life, von Schlachta has been researching the Anabaptists, with particular emphasis on the Hutterites. Her dissertation concentrated on the Hutterites of the late 16th and early 17th centuries. Her most recent book, *Täufer: Von der Reformation ins 21. Jahrhundert* [*Anabaptists: From the Reformation to the 21st Century*] was released in June 2020. Astrid von Schlachta is also president of the Mennonitische Geschichtsverein [Mennonite Historical Society, Germany] and the 500 Jahre Täuferbewegung 2025 Society which is preparing to commemorate the 500th anniversary of the Anabaptist Movement in 2025.

www.ingramcontent.com/pod-product-compliance
Lightning Source LLC
Chambersburg PA
CBHW041130110526
44592CB00020B/2750